COASTWI

ALAN ROSS was born in Calcutta in 1922 and spent his childhood in Bengal, arriving in an unfamiliar England at the age of seven. He was at Haileybury and St John's College, Oxford, before serving in the Royal Navy during the Second World War. Thereafter he worked for the British Council and from 1953 to 1972 was cricket correspondent for the *Observer*. He has been editor of the *London Magazine* since 1961 and publisher of London Magazine Editions since 1965. A wide variety of authors has appeared under the LME imprint including, Roy Fuller, Paul Theroux, Tony Harrison, Gavin Ewart, Graham Swift and Hugo Williams. Alan Ross's many other books include: *Death Valley*, which was a Poetry Book Society Choice; *Colours of War*, a study of war art 1939-1945; *Ranji*, the life of the Indian cricketer-prince; and two travel books about Corsica and Sardinia, *Time Was Away* and *The Bandit on the Billiard Table*, both of which are published as Harvill paperbacks. *Coastwise Lights*, which deals with his postwar life as cricket correspondent, publisher and man of letters, is the second of two classic volumes of autobiography. The first, *Blindfold Games*, which covers his early life and wartime experiences sailing on Arctic convoy duty, is also available as a Harvill Paperback.

Alan Ross

COASTWISE LIGHTS

COLLINS HARVILL
8 Grafton Street, London W1
1990

COLLINS HARVILL
William Collins Sons and Co Ltd
London · Glasgow · Sydney · Auckland
Toronto · Johannesburg

BRITISH LIBRARY CATALOGUING IN PUBLICATION DATA

Ross, Alan, *1922-*
Coastwise lights
I. English literature.
Biographies
I. Title
828'.91409

ISBN 0-00-272127-9

First published in Great Britain by Collins Harvill 1988
This paperback edition first published by Collins Harvill 1990

© Alan Ross 1988

Printed and bound in Great Britain by
William Collins Sons & Co. Ltd, Glasgow

For Jennifer, Jonathan and Victoria
and in memory of these friends

Swift shuttles of an Empire's loom that weave us main to main
The Coastwise Lights of England give you welcome back again.

RUDYARD KIPLING

CONTENTS

Preface   9

PART I   Two Painters   11

PART II   With Morgan to Baghdad   63

PART III   Drinkers and Dandies   99

PART IV   North Africa   145

PART V   *London Magazine* and Publishing   169

PART VI   Sussex Connections   189

PART VII   The Racing Game   227

PREFACE

I described in its Preface an earlier book, *Blindfold Games*, as being only incidentally autobiography, but more accurately "the raw material out of which I began to write poetry". The same principle applies here, at least as far as the autobiographical part is concerned. *Coastwise Lights* turns out mainly to be about friends – painters and writers – who were close to me and who have since died. I had not intended the book to take such a shape, but there it is.

Blindfold Games began in India and ended, after describing a Sussex adolescence, Oxford and five years in the Navy, in occupied Germany. It was about coming to terms with war and a hunger for writing replacing a passion for cricket.

The present volume takes the story from 1947 to 1978, when I returned to London after living in Sussex for twenty-five years. During most of this time I was working for the *Observer*, as well as taking over the *London Magazine* in 1961 and starting up as a publisher in 1965. As in *Blindfold Games* I have used poems written at the time as illustrations and to fill in a few gaps. Some relate to the text, others to relationships or derive from working journeys in Europe, Australia, Africa and the Caribbean.

A.R.

PART I

Two Painters

THE NEON LETTERS flicked on and off outside the window, LE JO KEY, the C missing. The name was all I knew, a Montparnasse nightclub, its external showcase decorated with racing paraphernalia – jockeys' silks, a whip – as background to champagne bottles and menus embellished with half-naked girls. I had been there once, on leave, two years earlier, but could remember little about it. Like most such excursions of the time, taken to escape the depressingness of occupied Germany, it dissolved in a haze of alcohol, leaving only hangover and vague recollections of women.

I had enough money for the purpose then, for the few days generally available. Now I had practically none, and anyway it was forbidden, in 1947, to take more than £25 out of the country.

I lay restless on my bed, waiting. The room, which cost five francs, was the size of a cabin, and the jokey neon when it came on filled the wall above the iron bed. The light was bright enough for shadow puppets. A smell of dust and lime trees mingled with those of Gitanes and garlic.

The room had no basin, only a tin bowl and a jug, and under the bed a cracked chamber pot decorated with vine leaves. Next door was a *toilette* of sorts, from whose ventilation panel above the cistern you could look into an apartment in the next building a few feet away.

I discovered this early on that sweltering August, for returning one evening with John Minton from the usual, but necessarily limited, round, I heard voices so close as I entered the lavatory that I thought someone was climbing the wall.

I stood up on the seat, expecting to be confronted by a plumber or burglar. Instead, within touching distance, I found myself a hidden spectator – the fourth wall – of a domestic scene played without clothes and apparently without plot. There were three characters, all of them naked. Nearest to me a white-bearded man, probably in his seventies, sat at a school-type desk studying a racing paper. In the middle of the room, stock-still, a plump, middle-aged woman appeared, in mid-stride, to be counting stitches as she knitted, strands of green wool mooring her to the ball at her feet. On a double bed in the far corner another man, bald, heavily muscled and tattooed, lolled against the pillows reading a *roman-policier*.

Apart from their nakedness, understandable in the heat and of no concern to themselves, it was scarcely a sight to hold the attention. Yet, if it had been the opening moment of a play, one's curiosity would have been aroused. To which, if either, of the men was the woman related, and were they related to each other?

I observed them for a few minutes, the older man staring as if hypnotized at the Deauville results, the woman quietly pacing up and down, her lips moving as her needles clicked, the man on the bed continuing to be absorbed in his book.

I was about to descend from my perch when, as if they were clockwork figures just wound up, each of them moved, disrupting the tableau effect and creating a series of new relationships. The student of form pushed up his specs, stretched and ambled over to fetch a can of beer. The thriller reader swung his legs off the bed, yawned and walked across to the sink in which he began vigorously to pee. The woman carried on with her knitting, walking back and forth.

A few minutes later the woman, for no apparent reason, leaned over the older man and proffered him, with the delicacy of the Duchess of Villars in the painting by Clouet, a cherry-coloured nipple. He looked up at her, unconcernedly deposited a foamy lick on her nearer breast, and went back to his paper.

The woman put her knitting down, pottered about for a minute or two in the corridor outside, and then joined the man on the bed, taking his book from him and laying it over his sex which rested like a half-submerged submarine between his thighs. He picked the book up without comment and continued to read. She turned her back on him and prepared for sleep. Back in my own room I continued to hear the rustle of paper and pages until I dozed off. I dreamed I was back at sea in No. 5 Mess, only the Bosun had become a woman, lewdly displaying herself on the lockers while we tried to read or sleep.

For the next week, while the heat lasted, variations of this tableau were performed. Few words were exchanged but the silent activities became more surreal, the woman demonstrating a marked sense of the incongruous, despite the indifference of her companions. One night she folded her knitting round the bald man's balls, as if making a bonnet for them, a piece of frivolity he dismissed with an impatient gesture, as if brushing away a mosquito. On another evening, after doing her ablutions, she walked around with her toothbrush sticking out of her bottom, inviting the old man to clean his teeth. He took them out and absent-mindedly did so, reading the while. She liked to drape her knickers over his racing paper, preventing him from reading. His response to this was to place them on his head and pat her buttocks consolingly.

I tried to interest Johnny Minton in these existential scenes, to which at different times Jarry, Beckett, Sartre and Delvaux appeared to have contributed, but the performers were not young enough to attract him. I, however, found myself thinking more and more about them as we wandered about Paris, speculating on what the night might reveal. Perhaps they were retired comedians or clowns, their bodies and routines so familiar to one another through long association that speech was no longer necessary. I began to get the impression that they were waiting for something, perhaps an engagement in a provincial city, or for some news – possibly of a criminal nature – that would activate them. They offered no clues as to their feelings or allegiances, though it seemed likely that the woman belonged nominally to the bald one. At the same time there was something ritualistic or sculpted about their behaviour, as if they were under pressure not to deviate from what had been laid down. The woman's attempts to introduce some levity to the proceedings cut no ice.

One evening I heard music and the woman laughing. She had tied a banana to the old man's crotch as he sat reading and was flicking it. The black mat between her own legs was adorned with a red rose. The bald man was absent, there was a gramophone playing, and she prodded the old one until he got up and executed a few steps, rubbing herself lasciviously against the banana. From time to time, like a dancing bear trained to improvise, he did a fancy shuffle or two on his own, his face expressionless. Then she sat down on his lap, put on his spectacles and imitated him studying the runners. He pushed her off gently and went on as before.

I never discovered what any of them did in the daytime. The flat appeared empty until the early evening, its shutters drawn. The weather cooled off, and when I next looked in on them they were all three clothed, sitting at the table, eating, drinking and even talking, the woman recounting some adventure and the two men grunting.

William Sansom told me a story of how, one particularly hot September, he had gone on his own to Venice to finish a novel. After a day or two he became conscious of frequent sluicing noises in the adjoining room, separated only by a connecting door. Putting his eye to the keyhole he found himself gazing at a large voluptuous blonde, whom he had already eyed with interest in the foyer, rubbing herself down after a shower. In the great heat the showering and naked perambulating were frequent. Eventually, distracted beyond endurance, Bill abandoned his attempts at work, an eye infection causing him to return early.

I continued to find my new neighbours consorting anarchically in my dreams with old mess mates: the woman transferring the red rose from her bush to the ear of old George Moulson of No. 5 Mess, the bald man running her knickers up the mast as a bizarre signal for entering harbour, the white-bearded fellow, now in oilskins and sou'wester, on the bridge reading the runners at Chantilly to an incredulous captain.

There was something in the room across the way that had merged in my mind with a scene from the war: the notion of waiting for something to happen, a torpedo to hit or a mere alteration of course, the reluctant participants irrevocably bound to one another yet locked apart in their own thoughts. The old man had something of Moulson's waddle; the woman of the Bosun's big-hipped shuffle, observed once as he came naked from the showers to the CPO's mess, the bald man of Smithy's indifference to the company and to his surroundings.

There was something, too, that reminded me of Eugene O'Neill, of a play set on board a derelict freighter; or was it from a novel by Traven? Whatever it was, those three figures, marooned in the heat, naked and silent, stirred a claustrophobic recollection in me that never entirely went away.

When finally Johnny and I left Paris for the south I had it fixed in my mind that just such a scene, a group static and confined under bare bulbs, held some associative significance. I was glad that nothing had been resolved, no indications given. The added dimension of nudity I put down to Paris and the weather, a reverse image of the external ice and battened-down fug that was our normal wartime condition.

That August of 1947 was memorable for its heat, Europe sluggish in its indolence. A few months earlier I had published *The Derelict Day*, my first volume of poems, all of them written during the preceding year in Germany. On the basis of that and some bits and pieces of prose, I received an Atlantic Award from the Rockefeller Foundation, one of half a dozen British writers – Robert Kee was another – to qualify by reason of war service and of work produced. The work produced was pretty sketchy in my case. The award was only £500 but it seemed a fortune at the time.

Before retiring my uniform I had presented myself at an officers' rehabilitation board, the function of which was to find suitable jobs for officers or suitable officers for jobs. They noted down my places of education, my naval duties, and such qualifications as I had, which were not many. The lack of a degree was unfortunate, they said, though of course many others had suffered similar interruption to their university careers. Had I thought of going back to Oxford and completing my course? Yes, I had thought of it but I had been away five years now and I wanted to get on. I had also hoped to play county cricket for a season or two, but now that chance had gone as well. If I had managed to get out of Germany six months earlier both might have been possible.

They were sympathetic and said they would get in touch. They never did.

The Rockefeller money had given me a year's grace. I rented a tiny house in Kinnerton Street for £8 a week, then a flat near the zoo, and finally some rooms in Elm Park Gardens which I shared with a girl who had been liaison officer on the Germany Under Control exhibition on which I had been working during my last weeks in the Navy.

It was cold, and my only really warm clothing was my naval officer's greatcoat, from the shoulders of which I had stripped the marks of rank; it reached almost to the ground. During the day I tried to write a novel without enough conviction and eventually it died of inanition. A sedentary existence, unless it is producing results, is lowering and I was not used to it, nor to the lack of exercise. By the early afternoon I was usually out of sorts, having wasted the whole morning with nothing to show for it. If I went to the pub I felt discontented and listless. Occasionally I was given books to review for *Tribune*, where T. R. Fyvel had succeeded George Orwell as literary editor. I wanted to write poetry but the war as a subject still occupied me and anyway I had enough sense to realize that writing poetry would not get me very far on its own.

I even began to think nostalgically of warship life; the friendships and good, cheap drinking, the movement and excitement. The boredom of it faded and the sea itself, often liverish-making and dreaded at the time, began to appear in a new light, unrealistically blue and romantic. The euphoria of slipping up the Harwich estuary at dawn, after a successful patrol, the hills magically green and the air intoxicating, was still recent enough for me to find my present way of living deadly and unpromising in comparison. Had I been able to write and known what to write I don't suppose I would have felt any of this. What I knew was that something real was slipping away from me and I could neither stop it nor replace it.

My infatuation for Soho life had more or less ended with the war. It seemed a dead, seedy place now, peopled by hangers-on and time-wasters. War and the influx of soldiery had provided it with vitality and variety, as well as ensuring a rapid change of faces. Now only a few of the old regulars – Julian Maclaren-Ross and Tambimuttu, Nina Hamnett and Sylvia Gosse, the Roberts Colquhoun and MacBryde – continued to turn up, and they were not particularly the ones I wanted to see. Julian's cigarette holder and Nina's tin money box had both lost their novelty and their gossip most of its fascination.

Still, for old times' sake, I went there once in a while, with Keith Vaughan and Johnny Minton, and now and again someone looked in who had briefly been a friend and was unrecognizable out of uniform, diminished as we all were, at least for the time being. It certainly wasn't fun any more, and efforts to make it appear so seemed hollow. There were a few bridge-playing cronies still around, from one or other of the Harwich destroyers or from Germany, and once a week we made up a four, the time passing very quickly then.

As the evenings lengthened, so did people begin to make excuses, finding better things to do, moving away or into different company. I asked Ronald Chesney, our First Lieutenant at Wilhelmshaven, to join us once, but the idea was not well received by the others and in any case he failed to turn up. Within a few years he would be dead, having been on the run after a double murder. He killed himself in a wood near Cologne.

Soon I took to spending afternoons at Lord's, hanging around the Tavern while Denis Compton and Bill Edrich scored hundred after hundred, making batting seem the easiest and most enjoyable thing in the world.

The idea that John Minton and I should do a travel book together must have been John Lehmann's. He had started the publishing house that bore his name the year before. The firm had a depressingly brief life but while it lasted it promised great things. The best of the new generation of Americans – Paul Bowles, Tennessee Williams, Merle Miller, Gore Vidal – and the French, German and Italian authors first published in *New Writing* added flavour to a list that soon included Elizabeth David's cookery books, a reprint series and

20

children's books illustrated by leading painters. Every book was beautifully produced, and many of them were designed by Keith Vaughan. John Minton had done the jacket for *The Derelict Day* and had also produced covers for *Penguin New Writing*, soon to be abandoned by its proprietor for no satisfactory reason.

I'm not sure what made us settle on Corsica, particularly. Was it part of the plan I had conceived in Germany for trawling the ports of Europe, down the Baltic to the Black Sea, or that other idea of following Nelson round the Mediterranean, Nelson being a hero we shared? Perhaps Nelson had something to do with it, or Boswell, or, most likely of all, Edward Lear, whose *Journal of a Landscape Painter* was published in 1868. At any rate, John Lehmann was in touch with the French Minister of Culture, Louis Joxe, who had agreed to help us with travel arrangements. It so happened he was abroad when we arrived in Paris, which was why we were kicking our heels in the heat awaiting his return.

John Minton was five years older than I was, a familiar face from wartime Soho, always laughing and joking. I remember him turning up at one of John Lehmann's parties wearing an Old Wellingtonian tie. Cuthbert Worsley, who had been a master at Wellington, where he had taught Gavin Ewart among others, asked him when he had been there. "Don't be silly, my dear," Johnny answered airily, "do I look as if I would have been there?" Cuthbert became extremely cross, and the more heated he became the more Johnny laughed.

The tie had, in fact, belonged to one of Johnny's brothers. Although his father, a solicitor, was of the Minton china family, there had apparently not been enough money around for all three sons to go to public school. Johnny had been sent to a preparatory school at Bognor and then to Reading School, leaving at the age of eighteen to go to St John's Wood Art School. When war broke out he had registered as a conscientious objector, later changing his mind and being

21

commissioned in the Pioneer Corps. He was released not long afterwards, because, or so he told me, he had confessed to his Colonel that he was a homosexual, a preference which, in the circumstances, put him under strain. It does not sound a very convincing reason, so he may have made it up. I don't think he ever saw much of his father, but his mother, after a divorce, had taken up with a taxi driver. Whether Johnny had an allowance from his father I don't know, but there was money somewhere, for Johnny inherited a fatal amount some time in the '50s.

By the time the Corsican idea came up Johnny had already shown at Roland, Browse and Delbanco and at the Lefèvre. He had recently moved from teaching book illustration at Camberwell to a similar job at the Central. During the last two years of the war he shared a studio with the Scottish painters Colquhoun and MacBryde; no rest cure, since they were quarrelling or drunk much of the time, but in 1946 he took a lease on two floors of a house in Hamilton Terrace and shared it with Keith Vaughan.

Their geographical territories were strictly observed. The raised ground-floor space, consisting of an airy, high-ceilinged room with double French windows opening on to a balcony and overlooking a large sloping garden, was Minton territory. Below stairs a boiler room, a bathroom and a kitchen, with Keith's much smaller studio-bedroom on the garden level, was Vaughan country. Apart from the fact that they were both painters and homosexual they had little in common. Johnny was mannered, frivolous in speech, compulsively gregarious, open-handed. Keith was reserved, self-contained, tidy in habit and mind, grumpy. Johnny behaved wildly and without inhibition, alternating between high spirits and physical exhaustion, always generous with his time. He liked to appear unserious, as though the whole art business was a lark. Keith, on the other hand, was miserly with his time, cross at any distraction, but, as the day wore on, he mellowed. Once

22

work was over he was the friendliest and most rewarding of companions, serious in the best sense, sharply observant and critical, but also funny. Not surprisingly, as the one grew more and more a creature of the night, attended, particularly after the money rolled in, by a larger and larger retinue of 'students', and the other remained selectively domestic, they came to see less and less of each other. I cannot remember them ever going out together.

Johnny and I set off for Paris in the middle of August. We planned to return via Dinard, where my father had bought a house and assumed the not onerous duties of Vice-Consul. He had spent forty years in India and his health had steadily deteriorated, to the point where his years of retirement brought him little pleasure. Without his work he seemed like a fish out of water, and since he had been obliged to leave most of his money in India, he and my mother lived in a more modest fashion than they had ever done before.

Every morning in Paris, before the lure of the *tableau vivant* drew me to my nocturnal perch, we made our way to Monsieur Joxe's Ministry. Finding nothing doing, we would continue on to the Bain Deligny, the swimming pool on the Seine, and spend the rest of the day there. Although Paris was comparatively empty the suffocating weather had resulted in the sun-bathing area's being so crowded that everyone had to lie body to body, head between someone else's legs. Visual intimacy between perfect strangers was often as close as between the most curious of lovers.

Cheap though our hotel was, our reserves began to run dangerously low. However, just in time, Monsieur Joxe was back in his office, a passage to Ajaccio was fixed up, and we were on the night train to Marseilles.

I had not, before we left London, ever spent any time alone with Johnny. He always seemed slightly uneasy on his own, as if questions might be put to him that he preferred not to consider. In a group anything personal, or untoward, could be deflected by banter. But now, at the start of our several weeks together, I came to realize in him a degree of melancholy that was both fleeting and profound.

It was not simply that his gaunt, El Greco-like features were of the kind that, unless animated, assumed a sadness bordering on the tragic. Or that the shape of his mouth, with its prominent teeth, meant that in repose, and especially when sleeping, his jaw tended to sag. These were physical attributes that had no real bearing on expression.

The melancholy was in his eyes, a look eloquent both of defeat and of loss. When he was not conscious of being observed, gazing perhaps through a window or into the distance or at nothing at all, he had the air of someone who had come to the conclusion that all hope was illusory, that whatever was worth attaining was already out of reach, beyond recall. He exuded this sense of desolation like a musk, and then, as soon as he snapped back into focus, almost as if the structure of the face itself had undergone change, or been reassembled, it was gone. He had the most mobile features imaginable and eyes that lit up or went out as suddenly as electric light bulbs.

At this time he was only thirty, a painter, mainly in watercolour or gouache, of romantic urban and rural landscapes in the manner of Samuel Palmer and the early Graham Sutherland. His oils were more linear and compressed; cubism given a particular English twist.

But in Corsica over the next month he began to develop a style completely his own, one which not only filled our book with wonderfully evocative drawings – harbours, mountains, village streets, fishermen – but which he was to use to brilliant effect in subsequent travels in Spain, Morocco, Norway and the West Indies. Almost every year between 1947 and 1956 he held a one-man show of watercolours, and except for the last of these, when the tide was turning against his way of painting, they were all immediate sellouts. His angular, bony draughtsmanship, reflective of his own physique, captured the essence of places, their picturesque aspect, with a skill and facility that only Edward Lear has matched in English romantic art. His gouaches had a natural grace and fluency that seemed devoid of effort, the colours ravishing. When, later, European art was under assault from the vigorous, brash, brush strokes of Pollock, Kline and de Kooning, these decorative qualities told against him. Johnny, only too well aware of the threat of New York-based abstract expressionism to prevailing taste, took to painting large pictures on heroic subjects – The Harbour, The Death of Nelson, The Death of James Dean – which earned him some notoriety, especially when Munnings, then President of the Royal Academy, abused them. He also painted vaguely cubist portraits of public figures like Dominguin and Elizabeth Schwarzkopf, but his oils, though well organized, never lost a certain stiffness. In watercolour and gouache he seemed absolutely himself, his art the natural expression of his personality.

At the time of our arrival in Corsica, Johnny had already made a mark as a painter of promise – someone in the line of Berman, de Chirico, Buffet – though he was not yet the well-known figure and object of interest to the press he was to become a few years later. He was also being taken up as an illustrator of books, doing *Le Grand Meaulnes* for Paul Elek and *Treasure Island* for John Lehmann. Soon he would be doing drawings for H. E. Bates's *The Country Heart* and Elizabeth David's *A Book of Mediterranean Food* and *French Country Cooking*.

I find it painful to re-read now what I wrote then. For some obscure reason, perhaps out of a genuine diffidence, I decided at the outset that "I" or "we" should not figure in the narrative, that Johnny and I should be invisible travellers, observing, experiencing, recording, but not intruding. It was the result, perhaps, of too literal an obeisance to Christopher Isherwood's method in *Goodbye to Berlin*, though his "I am a camera" technique did not preclude his own considerable involvement in the lives of his characters.

25

The consequence of this was that the landscape and the characters we met had to do all the work. It is a reasonable assumption that a book about Corsica should be about Corsicans and not about oneself, but in practice this leads to an inevitable distancing. The best travel books are nearly always as interesting for what the traveller tells us of his own experiences and feelings as for what he says about the country he travels through. I don't imagine there is another travel book in existence in which there is not a single use of the word "I".

Corsica was even hotter than Paris, but it had fresh air and sea. Arriving at Ajaccio at first light, the mountain-framed bay coming into brilliant focus as the battered old *Portugal* tied up alongside a palm-lined waterfront, I had my first view of the true Mediterranean since, ten years earlier, I had sailed as a schoolboy on the old Anchor line *Britannia* on my way to and from India.

Few feelings in the world equal that of coming in by sea to a foreign port for the first time. As often as not the city when one experiences it on land fails to live up to the dream mirage rising out of the horizon. Ajaccio itself scarcely passes the test, but when I think of exotic landfalls over the years – Dubrovnik, Cape Town, Papeete, Bombay, Naples, Sydney, Jakarta, Pusan – they cannot quite compete with the first excitement and revelation of Ajaccio.

We spent some days in Ajaccio roaming about, stunned by the heat, but looking at churches, visiting bars, and generally trying to get the hang of the place. Bonaparte, who was born here, had no great interest in or love for the place, though in exile on Elba he expressed nostalgia for the warm scent of the maquis on the hills above Ajaccio.

Nevertheless, his reputation brooded over the whole island, his name lent to every second bar, café, street, bakery, in one form or another – Bar au 1er Consul, Café Napoléon, Rue Bonaparte. Shortly before Napoleon was born the Genoese, who had ruled the island, with short interruptions, since the eleventh century, sold the sovereignty of the island to France. The Corsicans, not for the first time in their history, fought fiercely for their independence, but the rebels were eventually subdued and in 1790 Corsica became a department of France. Not long afterwards the Corsican leader Pasquale Paoli enlisted British help, British troops landed, and for a bizarre two years Corsica became part of the British Empire. Soon the British found themselves no more welcome than their predecessors, and reluctantly, in 1796, the Corsicans accepted their dependency on France.

We quickly discovered that the spirit of independence was by no means dead. There was a French *préfet* as nominal head of the Government, a French general commanding the garrison in Ajaccio, and a French admiral at the naval base. The Corsicans resented not only their loss of identity and the slight to their pride but also the fact that they were neglected. From time to time they let off bombs and fired shots, especially at elections. The present mayor of Ajaccio was a communist, but for every slogan daubed on the walls advocating *Votez Communiste* there was another saying *Vive de Gaulle*.

What we learned, talking to fishermen, barmen, petty officials in local government, was that political philosophies were an irrelevance, and that as long as the island was administered from Paris the Corsicans would limit their involvement to serving their own interests. The talk in the bars was of the prices of sugar, oil and fish in Marseilles, of the cost of cocaine. Ajaccio, as we grew more familiar with it, seemed tense and indolent at the same time, a furtive city where people whispered in corners and strange objects changed hands.

The mineral wealth of the island, its natural resources, had long been allowed to go to waste. There was neither the labour to exploit it nor the incentive. The young men preferred to leave and try their luck on the mainland.

Despite its romantic beauty Ajaccio had the air of a place

living on its nerves, steeling itself for a revolutionary gesture that had no hope of succeeding.

All that has changed now. The indolence, partly historic, partly malarial, has receded, and if independence on the islanders' terms has not materialized they may never really have wanted it. Political activists have, from time to time, threatened revolt, but a few bombs here, a shooting there, and the drama subsides, the summer takes over. When we were there Corsica was a sleepy island submerged in its past; now, with the establishment of new resorts and hotels, it is prosperous and thriving. But still, almost through habit, the bombs go off, the random political murder takes place.

As we set off on our way across the island to Porto-Vecchio there were no foreigners in the bus other than ourselves. Our fellow passengers were soldiers going on leave, some nuns, a Dominican priest, old women in black clutching loaves, chickens, wine and peaches.

That first precipitous climb into the mountains, past donkeys in straw hats nodding under pine trees, the cactus giving way to olive, made me realize how quickly Johnny could work. Asleep most of the time in the bus, his head lolling on my shoulder, no sooner had we stopped at some mountain village than he was up and out with his pen and drawing board. Within ten minutes, the length of a halt, he had done enough ground work for the finishing touches to be added that same evening.

Day after day, as we sweated into dusty bays or rode laboriously into villages perched below the skyline, he produced his quota of beautiful drawings: harbours, fishermen, fruit markets, churches, walled towns, cemeteries. Later, he made illustrations for the portrait poems I wrote on Corsican travellers and celebrities – Napoleon, Edward Lear, Boswell.

It was rugged travel; the hotels where we stayed were basic and often dirty. We lived on bread, cheese, figs, pastis and wine. The bus journeys were slow and suffocating, with long stops for no particular reason. One day we would be languishing in the humid heat of an estuary, the next exhilarated by sweet mountain air, waking to forests and mountains. We never saw an English person, and hardly any French, except at Calvi and Île-Rousse towards the end of our trip.

Wherever we went, to Cargèse or Bonifacio, Corte or Corbara, Olmeto or Bastia, there was something to remind one of Genoese or Greek occupiers, of local heroes like Sampiero and Paoli or extravagant adventurers like Theodor von Neuhoff, Corsica's only crowned king, who ended up in a debtors' jail in London and was buried in the churchyard of St Anne's, Soho. The stone at his head reads: "Near this place is interred Theodore, King of Corsica, who died in this parish, Dec: 11th, 1756, immediately after leaving the King's bench prison, by the benefit of the act of insolvency: in consequence of which, he registered his Kingdom of Corsica for the use of his creditors."

We were overconscious perhaps of island sloth and corruption, of the drug-running and fatalism that seemed the legacies of a colonial past. Life, for all but the old, took place somewhere else. Quite soon one learned that these claustrophobic feelings were not unique to Corsica but the common malaise of country people almost everywhere, from Italy to India. The cinema and television had made the bright lights of the city appear glamorous and there were no bright lights in the hill villages of Corsica.

Instead, at every turn of the road, there were views of breathtaking magnificence, the mountains on one side, the sea a milky green or dazzling blue on the other. The villages we stayed in were sad, dusty places, scarcely more than bus stops; there would be a fly-blown café under plane trees, a neglected bar, a locked church usually scrawled with communist graffiti. Once out of them the spirits immediately lifted in the marvellous air.

Heavily influenced by Graham Greene's *The Lawless Roads* and *Journey Without Maps*, I think I was perhaps too inclined to see Corsica in terms of defeated priests, corrupt politicians and saintly monks. There were all of these, but there were lively, bustling waterfronts, too, and in the northwest a stretch of coast that belonged in spirit to the south of France.

It was at Corbara, wedged into the high peaks behind the resort of Île-Rousse, that we had our only encounter with the contemplative life. We had come for Johnny to make a drawing of the Dominican monastery whose pure white rectangle, a change from the sugary pink of the village churches, we had seen from the coast road out of Calvi. The world seemed shut out by its steep walls; the entrance and chapel were set on the far side of the building, almost into the rock. At first glance it seemed deserted, a place of high winds, sheer fall and screaming birds. I wandered round a small cemetery, surrounded by cypresses, and looked at the inscriptions on the simple tombstones – "Ici repose Antonio", "Soeur Thérèse 1879–1940" – while Johnny roughed out his drawing.

Within an hour he had almost done. There seemed no way to look into either the courtyard or the chapel, for all exterior doors were padlocked and windows shuttered, but we rang the bell just in case. Nothing happened for some minutes and we were about to leave when a key rattled in one of the heavy doors and a small, plumpish figure, his jovial, bespectacled face covered in grey stubble, emerged, apologizing for his slowness.

Père Obein had been at Corbara for more than thirty years. The wind apparently never stopped blowing, a warm, dry wind from Algeria that got on your nerves and also frequently rang the bell. Since they had so few visitors they rarely bothered to answer it. Inside the cloisters and out of the wind the atmosphere was altogether friendlier. Red roses and geraniums softened the harsh glare of the white walls, and the sun, slanting through pillars, warmed the stone corridors.

For the rest of the morning Père Obein took us through the various chapels, refectories and cellars, recounting the sad history of the place in a gentle voice as he did so. The site had been chosen in the fifteenth century for use as an orphanage but it had not been operating long when some visiting Obsevatin fathers took a fancy to it and decided to take it over. A monastery was constructed in its place by Franciscan monks and for three hundred years they had studied and prayed there in peaceful seclusion.

Then in 1792 the Revolutionary authorities had expelled them, burning their books. The gardens were sold off in lots to local families and all the buildings, except for the church, were allowed to fall into ruin. Within fifty years it had become a wilderness.

In 1857 two *frères prêcheurs* obtained consent to rebuild the monastery, opening a school on the premises. Shortly afterwards Father Bouvard, the Prior, was assassinated in the church by Paris Communards. Italians briefly replaced the French Dominicans but no sooner had the French returned than, in 1903, a law was passed against brotherhoods. The nine monks there at the time were obliged to leave and sell up, the place once again being left to rot. Since then it had been used variously as a military and civilian jail, and to house prisoners of war.

It was Père Obein who confirmed our feeling about the island, the abandoned villages and general neglect. "The only Corsica that still lives is in France," he said, "split up into hundreds of separate people, who only come back here to die."

A rumour that the place was going to be converted into an institution came to the rescue of Corbara as a retreat. The villagers became alarmed and pleaded that the monks should be allowed to return, vandalized and derelict though the buildings were. The authorities got in touch with the Order and in ones and twos they came back.

The rebuilding was put in hand and now there were twelve

monks, their work alternating between preaching in the mountain villages and running the monastery. Everything they ate they produced themselves, they had cows and sheep, and they made their own wine. Perhaps we would like to try some of it, he asked. He led the way into a long, cool cellar lined with barrels and stacked with wine racks. A winepress at the far end reached to the stone ceiling.

We drank from amber, fluted glasses, the wine deliciously cold, faintly raw. On our way out Père Obein pointed to an opening in the cloisters barred by three rusty cylinders. Defaulting priests were imprisoned there, he said. They slept on a stone floor and received communion through the bars. Near the great entrance gate we heard low voices coming through a half-open window. There were some novices studying there, Père Obein told us, and every day philosophical and religious discussions were held under the guidance of a senior monk. Had they not been in residence just then he would have asked us to stay. But with the novices to be looked after it would have been too much for the four nuns who cooked, washed and cleaned for the community. It was very restful, he said; complete silence except for readings from the Bible at meal times. We must come back.

It was a tempting prospect: peace and seclusion, time to read and write, no distractions. We said our goodbyes, and once the gate had clanged behind us the wind hit us, as if we were on the bridge of a galleon in a gale. The sea and the life of the coast seemed to belong to a different world. We picked our way down the narrow path that lay like a parting in the thick scalp of undergrowth, the sweet air giving way at every step to dust and sweat. From up here the island seemed to swing at its moorings.

We often talked of Père Obein, then and later. His gentleness of voice, his obvious feeling for the good life in all its aspects, his calm, all combined to make an impression on us, so much so that he became a kind of touchstone for future behaviour. "What would Père Obein say?" became an admonishment at times of crisis.

For the next few months, after we had returned to London, Johnny's drawing of Corbara was pinned over my bed: the path leading up through vines and cactus, the peaks above sawing at the blueness, the monastery clamped on to its plateau with the spire of the chapel just breaking the skyline. Then it went off to the printer and when it came back disappeared, like a hundred other drawings from the book, given away, or made off with by stray visitors, or simply lost in the muddle of an increasingly frenzied and chaotic life.

Johnny shared Lear's feeling for the picturesque, as he did much else; his eye for the essential features of a landscape, his facility and inability to make an ugly mark, his alternating gregariousness and gloom. But while Lear's art, wherever he found himself, inclined to the tentative and suggestive, a delicate product of dawn and dusk sketching, Johnny drew at high noon; the images were bolder, the shadows deeper, the colours brighter. Where Lear's watercolours of the island tend to the languid, Johnny's have energy and high spirits. It was partly a matter of temperament, partly seasonal – Lear was in Corsica in early summer, before the weather had settled. Clattering up and down hills in a two-horse carriage in the rain he not surprisingly found Corsica a melancholy place, the people drably dressed, "the land of the *Helix tristis*, the melancholy snail," he called it. At the end of a month, by which time Lear was thankfully back in Cannes, he had amassed more than 300 drawings and written a detailed if rather pedestrian journal. Johnny's method of working was not dissimilar: rough sketches on the spot, to be worked up in a hotel room later.

33

We returned in the early autumn, enjoying ourselves at Calvi and then flying from Ajaccio to Marseilles-Marignane. Calvi, where reputedly Columbus was born and Nelson lost his eye, is dominated by its huge Genoese fortress, but it is not a place where the past weighs on one. Rather, as the most convenient port of access from Nice, it is a haunt of smugglers and the idle rich. A number of White Russians were there then, running bars and nightclubs, and the town had an air of desperate gaiety. The beach was beautiful and the waterfront, with pink-washed houses, palm trees and striped awnings, boats with names like *Angèle* and *Michèle*, had a postcard prettiness. But here, too, the older inhabitants spoke of Corsica as an abandoned place, sunk in ennui. "*Mais tout reviendra*," said the burly Caucasian proprietor of Keripoff's, "*doucement*." And so it has.

One night we dined, under the stars and to the sound of Corsican guitars playing their *lamentos*, with Count Michel de Buisseret, not long returned from Buchenwald. The war had seemed mercifully behind us, but now it was brought up close once more and our survival seemed miraculous.

We were reminded of it again on our last day in Ajaccio, when, our plane delayed, we made a final round of the town – the house in the semi-slum of the Rue St Charles where Napoleon the First, Emperor of the French, was born, entry sixteen francs, and not far away the birthplace of Danielle Casanova, the young communist leader who was tortured to death at Auschwitz. A small plaque records her achievements, encouraging the youth of the island to follow her example on the way towards "*les lendemains qui chantent*".

Yet already, with the last war scarcely over, the tensions had begun to build up towards another one.

Cactus

Like orators declaiming or the grotesque
rubbery silhouettes of boxers, the prickly
paws fondle and miss the blue husk
of the day, already grown hot and sickly.

Below where they puncture and point
on the smoking hills, the harbour rides
securely under prints of coral and scent.
Boats turn over the sun on their sides.

Only the cactus hints with its nervous
shadows that Time is, unnoticed, away
on its own – a guest without fuss
who has left a hole in the day

by his absence and a growing alarm
that somewhere, northward in Europe,
away from the shade of indolent palms,
absurd orators, like cacti, strangle our hope.

Boswell on Tour

Armed with letters, he arrived, an Army –
the island, his terrain, was food for knowledge,
its people Characters, its noble General, God;
they thought him very eminent or balmy
– instead he balanced somewhere near the edge.

The scenery was nice, like murals, but no more,
a setting for an opera, or a landscape

suitable for love – and, as it happened, war.
The fight went to his head like wine,
the brand of liberty was his own design.

He found himself a hero, wrote his speeches
every day in notebooks, and preserved an awe
about him like a prophet – the best leeches
tended him when sick; he reached the shore.
They thought him all the while a secret envoy.

But everything he found, he could employ
later in books, in epigrams at after-dinner talks,
or earnestly let loose at Johnson on their walks.
As well he studied causes, histories, facts;
conscientiously he unearthed motives from their acts.

He got his views from all the best-briefed sources –
talked art with Paoli, the army with Marbœuf;
he even studied cattle and the local horses,
made notes on *moufflon*. There remained one thorn
– the Emperor Buonaparte was not yet born.

Guidebooks

Some things can still be learned, like dates;
the points of interest on the route, the best
hotels, the famous heroes with their tragic fates,
the types of landscapes and the ruined towers.
But guidebooks cannot tell you all the rest.

The real life goes on somewhere else, away
from lidos on the beach or staged, romantic ruins;
the picture postcards have their coloured say
in harbours bright with boats and sailing churches.
But life escapes and leaves them in the lurch.

36

They do not conjure up the smells or dirt,
the children's sores who idle near the bay;
nor say that here, beneath a bloodstained shirt,
a man's heart stopped through lack of human pity.
The personal details, like indecencies, are wrapped away.

They might admit, in tones of conversation,
that these fields rotted through a lack of work,
while back at home big business crucified the nation,
and people died in half-forgotten swamps or hills
through lack of means to fight the plague that kills.

But on the printed page the words are dead,
with no more meaning than the slogan scrawled
in chalk for sold-out leaders in the village halls.
The real life went dry inside a peasant's head
who died in war to write his name upon these walls.

Hill Donkeys

The flies hang in haloes round their heads,
or else deliberately walk across the muzzle
of their faces, contemptuous of the idle
flick they shiver out beneath their bridle
– for even when they work or softly nuzzle
into reeds, they're less important than the dead.

Indeed, they seem no more than patient
slaves, ordinary beasts whose overloaded backs
are used to suffering, but which never crack
through strain or knowledge of a hidden bent.
Only their nervous, immensely elegant feet
give them away – and picking their delicate
path through rocks, they betray their defeat.

Lear in Corsica

He took a rubber bath, his Suliot, and his gifts;
found friends and beauty but could not find romance
except in books; he waited on the highway as for lifts
but saw no pistol pointed at his head;
regretful, though relieved, he wrote "Romance is dead".

He packed his Nonsense up, like love, inside a box;
instead he courted Views, the ilex groves, the sea,
but, always careful, stopped to change his socks
when caught in storms and could not quite get in –
he travelled in a coach, but had no sense of Sin.

For, fifty-six, his comfort had become a vice,
his work dependent on his sleep and board;
and all the while he kept his verse on ice,
wrote prose, a little drab, to pass the time;
but was always happiest with a secret rhyme.

The island was a drink he drained of pleasure,
made daily drawings, sketches, journals, notes,
which later he developed and engraved at leisure
and filled a book with copious facts and charts.
But somehow drama evaded him in all his arts.

While, back in London, Johnny began preparing his drawings
for our book I looked around for a flat. Meanwhile I dossed
down in the boiler room of 37 Hamilton Terrace. I had
intended to stay only a few days but in the end I was there for
the best part of a year. One of the reasons was that my
application for a job at the British Council – without much
hope of success, since I had no degree – had resulted in an
interview and then an offer to edit a newsletter. This was a
not dissimilar affair from *The Pied Piper*, journal of Naval Party
1738, which I had edited in Germany. Its main purpose was

to keep former British Council scholars, research students and distinguished visitors in touch with each other and to publicize their activities. Since I had to turn up at Grosvenor Square by nine-thirty and rarely left before seven – regular evening receptions were held for the benefit of foreign students – there was not much time for flat-hunting.

The months at Hamilton Terrace provided a rewarding insight into two totally contrasting personalities and two quite different kinds of painter. As it happened, though it was Johnny who offered me the room, it was Keith of whom I began to see more. I don't know whether he welcomed my presence – unlikely, since his instinctive reaction to anything was always negative – but as Johnny was nearly always out in the evenings or surrounded by acolytes, it was with Keith that I usually had supper when I was in. Since I had no cooking facilities of my own, and in any case could scarcely boil an egg, I was dependent on the goodwill of both of them.

In one of his journal entries not long after we had settled in for the winter Keith wrote this:

> One of my big mistakes during the last two years has been trying to model my behaviour on Johnny – to emulate his debonair, easy irresponsibility. As though his success with people in this way could somehow be passed on to me, like an infection. It was always easier to tag along in his wake than strike out on my own. Now my growing resistance to his way of life (of which I disapprove but also envy) takes the form of making me peevish and morose, and thinking less well of him than he deserves. Since it is impossible for me just to live naturally in his ambience I should, of course, pack up and clear out. But what exactly is my way of life? Do the people I would like to know simply not exist – or do they exist but not here – or do they exist here and now and I, through some defect in myself, fail to make contact with them?

39

This problem obsessed Keith up to the last days of his life, a life ended, as was Johnny's, by his own hand.

In the meantime, while Johnny enjoyed social and commercial success, travelling each year to the Caribbean, North Africa or Spain, and filling portfolios with succulent drawings and watercolours, Keith dug himself in. His various romantic attachments seemed to cause him more distress than pleasure, though, unlike Johnny, he was naturally attracted to homosexuals rather than heterosexuals. Whereas Johnny made light of everything, Keith brooded, rather old-maidish in his habits, confiding his resentments, fantasies and general observations on art and life to his voluminous notebooks. From time to time he did break out, cruising Soho and returning drunk, with or without bedfellow. But these were rare occurrences, and when later a longstanding relationship developed it brought frustration and irritation rather than contentment.

Johnny soon moved from the Central to the Royal College, acquiring a new circle of friends and becoming even more frenetic. "I thought last night", Keith wrote perceptively in his journal entry of 25 December 1948, "that Johnny's use of life might be compared to a Tibetan's use of a prayer wheel. A circuit of activity is revolved with monotonous persistence in the simple belief that disaster can thereby be avoided and some lasting gain acquired. Almost every kind of experience can be tasted, but the revolutions are so quick that nothing can be grasped or savoured."

It was impossible to be in Keith's company long without becoming aware of his natural gravity and critical intelligence – the latter of a wry, dismissive kind. Once warmed up he was full of speculative humour, jokes and self-mockery. He was more widely read than Johnny, and more questioning, and when he talked about painting it was as someone who thought long and hard, not only about technical problems but about the relevance of art to every aspect of living.

Johnny too raised questions about the whole business of

being a painter, but in a different, jesting way. When he died, of a mixture of drink and sleeping pills – whether intentionally taken or otherwise was never quite clear – Keith observed in his journal entry of 25 January 1957:

> The one outstanding thing about him was that he was always so very much *alive*. He was never, as some people, half in love with death. But he was in love with destruction. And I can't help feeling that in destroying finally himself, this was meant to be just another unconsidered spontaneous act, a gesture which was not really intended to end in death. . . .
>
> Johnny will, I suppose, become a sort of legend now. After the rather dreary and desperate last three years of his life are forgotten, one will remember the scintillating creature one knew before. He was profligate in everything – with his affections, his money, his talents, and with all his warmth and charm essentially destructive. He turned everything into a joke and a subject for laughter. People never stopped laughing in his presence. "What does it all *mean*", he would repeat year after year, without really wanting to know the answer.

"What does it all *mean*?" That, alas, in the decade between our return from Corsica and the despairing overdose in Apollo Place, where after leaving Hamilton Terrace he had bought a house, became Johnny's habitual manner of greeting, a cliché, accompanied by waving of arms, intended to ward off any kind of normal conversation between friends. For no sooner were the words uttered than he was off.

They were, in fact, the last words I heard him speak, outside the V. & A., when we chanced to pass in the street a few months before his death. He stopped briefly, delivered the only too familiar rhetorical question, and hurried away, in flight both from an old friend and from himself. Michael Middleton, who had shared a studio with Michael Ayrton and Johnny in

Paris the summer before the war, described, in the catalogue to the Arts Council memorial exhibition held a year after Johnny's death, "the scarecrow figure with its loping, fevered stride, head down, chin stuck into chest, every fibre intent on getting wherever he was bound; the lantern face under the shock of hair, its extraordinary gravity in repose and its total re-creation in gaiety; the exuberant clowning into which was channelled, increasingly and defensively, a perpetual crackle of nervous energy".

There were, despite their essential differences, certain similarities of background between Keith and Johnny. In both cases younger brothers died tragically early, Keith's in 1940 as a pilot in the RAF, when Keith himself was a registered conscientious objector working with the St John's Ambulance. For a person prone to guilt feelings such a loss must have been overwhelming. Both Johnny's and Keith's fathers were absent during their formative years, through inclination in the former case, through death in the latter. Although neither had relationships with women they were homosexuals of quite different kinds; Johnny, so it seemed to me, socially and emotionally, and Keith sensually.

After I moved out of the boiler room to a flat even nearer to Lord's – my mate an exceptionally beautiful girl of Anglo-Polish origins, who, always late for her work as a model, used to weave down St John's Wood Road like a kind of motorized goose – I rarely saw Johnny except at parties. It was hard to imagine having lunch or dinner with him; he was too restless for that. He seemed never to change, simply to become more cynical, a self-confessed racketeer in art. Yet only at the very end, when he suddenly decided to leave the Royal College and concentrate on stage design, did his work show any falling off. It was simply that, as an abstract international style began to develop and figuration of any kind tended to be regarded as obsolete, Johnny increasingly found himself in a limbo between the avant-garde and the academic. Those who held their

42

ground like Francis Bacon and Lucian Freud came through, and so, of course, would Johnny have done. But his nerve failed him, his confidence evaporated and his plunge into drink and tranquillizers became more and more hectic. Aptly, his last public work was his set for *Don Juan in Hell* at the Royal Court, done shortly before his death.

With Keith I never lost touch. When, after our son Jonathan was born in 1953, we moved to Sussex, he frequently came down for weekends, beetling along the lane under the Downs in his open Morris Minor. He kept this car until his death, by which time it must have been twenty years old. He came and stayed with us in Ischia one September, a fellow guest of Cyril Connolly. The pair of them sat in total silence in the back of my open car, staring ahead or outwards like body-guards, each incapable of small talk or of making the first move. "What a nice person Keith is," Cyril typically remarked later, not having addressed a word to him for two weeks.

From Ischia Keith and I slowly drove back north, hugging the coast. Johnny would have wanted to stop and draw, but Keith had no such inclinations. We spent a night in Turin, dining in the magnificent restaurant of the Principi di Piemonte, and another at the Poste et Lion d'Or in Vézelay, after visiting the great Basilica Ste-Madeleine, a vision that drew from Keith a reluctant grunt. We lunched in autumn sunshine on the banks of the Yonne and I dropped him off in Paris.

Another year Keith joined us in Aegina. He wrote in his journal: "Not sure of the day but it doesn't matter. All days the same. Stillness and heat and the sea like distilled water. Bathing at Moni. Gleam of amphorae deep among rocks. Ouzo at the harbour in the evenings. Brown boys and pink boats loaded with dark green melons. Fish suppers on the terrace

43

overlooking the grey pistachio trees. Barrels of retsina, pine branches stuffed in the bung holes. Bill Sansom here with magnesia round his lips."

The magnesia was for chronic indigestion, and often left a white rim round Bill's mouth as if he had a moustache or had been eating chalk. I remember a story of Leonard Rosoman's of how, one night on some joint assignment to write and illustrate an article on the nudist island off Le Lavandou, Leonard had woken up to find Bill lying stark naked on the other bed and covered in what seemed a thick coating of cement. In some alarm and thinking Bill had contracted a horrifying disease, leprosy perhaps, Leonard switched on the light. It turned out that Bill, maddened by mosquitoes, had smeared toothpaste over himself from head to foot which had dried out to form a white cracked crust.

That same month Keith and I drove round the Peloponnese, Corinth, Nauplia, Epidaurus, Mycenae, Tirens. "Difficult to imagine the neurotic misery of Elektra in such an open air setting" he observed – rather unrealistically, given his own neuroses. "Two vast sweeps of mountain rise to the north and south and Mycenae crouches on the web of rock between."

Travelling with Keith was agreeable, although there was little he did not view with asperity. He rarely made drawings on the spot and when he did they seemed, in comparison to the virtually realized sketch that Johnny used so rapidly to do, rather feeble and fumbling. He had no great facility, but when he was drawing in earnest – as in his Iowa river drawings and those he made in Donegal in 1958 – the impress was firm and the structure solid.

I had never found Johnny's homosexuality obtrusive when I was abroad with him. Keith, however, was always on the look-out, which made me feel vaguely uneasy that my presence might deter potential lovers. It never affected his manners, but I became aware on our various travels together that after we

44

had said good night he would often slip out of the hotel, returning later with some boy he then had to smuggle in. I was apprehensive, because there was a sadistic as well as a masochistic streak in Keith, which his later and more private journals made only too clear. When I tackled him about the risks he was taking he made light of it, but I continued to have visions of an officious manager turning him out of the hotel in the middle of the night and probably me as well.

In 1962 Keith had a large retrospective at the Whitechapel. The Hamilton Terrace arrangement had come to an end some years before Johnny's death and Keith was now in Belsize Park, sharing his flat with Ramsay McClure, who, at that time, was designing window displays at an Oxford Street store. I remember Ramsay as being nondescript in appearance, slightly built and balding, his voice gentle with a faint Scottish accent. He appeared on the surface undemanding, unobtrusive and placid, but the honeymoon, such as it was, did not last. Before long Ramsay, either by his very presence or because of his acquiescent, dependent nature, was visibly getting on Keith's nerves.

Soon they acquired a cottage at Harrow Hill, in Essex, a small village to which Michael Ayrton and his wife had recently moved. Ramsay was banished there for most of the week, joined sometimes by Keith's mother, a tiny, busy and determined woman who increasingly became another source of irritation to him. Keith referred to his mother in his journal as a "controlled hysteric", but as far as one could see she was simply overprotective and managing, though possibly bird-brained as well. Ramsay, in his exile, took to cooking and gardening, but left alone so much he also took to the bottle. Aware that he annoyed Keith, he came to behave so unnaturally that it was impossible to be in a room with them both and not feel the strain.

45

The Whitechapel show, organized by Bryan Robertson, marked perhaps the high point of Keith's career. The example of de Stael in the mid fifties and the effect on Keith of certain American abstract painters – hitherto much despised – had suggested how figurative painting could come to terms with abstractionism, gaining tension and compression without compromise. Keith never lost his preoccupation with the male nude, depersonalizing it to such an extent that it became an integral part of its background, but after his visit to America in 1959 and his term as Resident Painter at Iowa State University he shed most of the neo-romantic mannerisms and symbols earlier associated with him and others of his generation, like John Craxton and Michael Ayrton.

Of all those who moved in and out of abstractionism Keith made the most successful transition. He lost nothing of his identity, simply merged it in pictorial compositions every one of which was as demonstrably his work as the bathers, wrestlers and fishermen of the '50s. His landscapes – empty beaches, untenanted orchards, rocky valleys, bare cliffs – acquired a new strength and ruggedness, reflective not only of solitude but also of defiance.

Keith was by nature a stoic and fatalist. A stocky figure, he was immensely strong and also attractive, until he began to lose his hair in his late forties so that he ended up looking like Verlaine. If Johnny Minton's physical characteristics were reflected in his painting, then certainly Keith's were as well, in a less obvious way.

The Whitechapel show was a revelation to most people, though, as Bryan Robertson observed, Keith lacked a clearly identifiable public, a situation to which he contributed by his own reclusiveness. His paintings of male assemblies and studies of adolescents naturally provided him with collectors as much attracted by their subject matter as by their manner and formal quality. But such paintings also shut him off from others who, with more perseverance, might have found reward in the power, complexity and suggestiveness of his technique. His landscapes were no obstacle, and some of his smaller gouaches, whether of English country scenes, the American Midwest or North Africa, are as seductive and accessible as any pictures of their period. But in the oils there is always – in a way rarely evident in a Minton painting or in the work of other contemporaries – a sense of drama and conflict, of the painter struggling to impose himself on recalcitrant materials. The completed work had to be wrestled into submission, the painter being in no doubt as to the arduousness of the process or the gravity of the issues.

This concentrated brooding over philosophical and technical matters gave all Keith's work a highly-charged atmosphere, so that one had the sense of being present at crucial and momentous deliberations. Yet there was nothing portentous or pretentious about him; rather the reverse. The essential seriousness of the concerns that were at the heart of his work was offset by a dry, no-nonsense manner and a total lack of illusion. The sweetness of character indicated by his own particular smile and the charm he exuded in his lighter moments – which were many – may not often have got into his painting, but the sensuousness was always evident. Few modern painters, in any case, convey whatever gregarious and sociable characteristics they may possess, the act of painting being a solitary one and usually more reflective of interior tensions than of general good will.

The Vaughan journals that I published in 1966 as one of the first books issued by my newly founded firm (others were Julian Maclaren-Ross's *Memoirs of the Forties*, Barbara Skelton's *Born Losers*, T. C. Worsley's *Flannelled Fool* and Bernard Spencer's *Collected Poems*) and the later extracts printed in the *London Magazine* after Keith's death are both revealing and tragic. They are revealing for the light they shed on a painter's character, and, to a lesser extent, working methods, and they are tragic for the contrast they expose between the public

47

face and the private misery. A dozen people must have thought they knew Keith well – Prunella Clough, his doctor Patrick Woodcock, Robert and Veronica Gosling, and myself among them – but none of us, I think, realized the isolation and sense of despair in him that the entries of his last years indicate.

It was, of course, partly his own fault. A natural diffidence, reinforced by a reluctance to waste time, made him settle for booze and music alone at home rather than accept invitations or invite someone over. "I seem to resemble some primitive form of life," he wrote, "an amoeba perhaps, which lives almost entirely off its own inner resources, hermaphroditic, unstable, able to take in only minute amounts of nourishment from outside and that with difficulty."

The two major exhibitions of the '60s at the Whitechapel – his own 1962 retrospective and the 1964 New Generation show – affected him in different, equally disturbing ways. About his own work he wrote:

> The strange thing about a retrospective is the appearance of orderly planned progression, as though the whole thing has been foreseen from the start. Whereas at the time each painting was just another attempt to solve the same problem. The results in each case defined the limits of one's ability, not the measure of one's intentions. The fact that these limits can just be seen to be slowly extending is the most reassuring evidence that one is still alive . . . Afterwards the difficulty is to persuade oneself that it was not a posthumous exhibition. The problem – my problem – is to find an image which renders the tactile physical presence of a human being without resorting to the classical techniques of anatomical paraphrase. To create a figure without any special identity (either of number or gender) which is unmistakably human, imaginative without

48

being imaginary. Since it is impossible to conceive a human form apart from its environment, an image must be found which contains the simultaneous presence and interpenetration of each. Hence the closer and closer interlocking bombardment of all the parts, like electrons in an accelerator, until the chance collision, felt rather than seen, when a new image is born.

The relevance of this technical problem, as he saw it, to the art of his time was struck a damaging blow two years later. Returning from the Whitechapel he had a horrifying inkling of what it felt like to be superseded.

After all one's thought and search and effort to make some sort of image which would embody the life of our time, it turns out that all that was really significant were toffee wrappers, liquorice allsorts and ton-up motorbikes . . . I understand how the stranded dinosaurs felt when the hard terrain, which for centuries had demanded from them greater weight and effort, suddenly started to get swampy beneath their feet. Over-armoured and slow-witted they could only subside in frightened bewilderment.

He was not alone in this feeling. Like most others of my age, for whom the war had been the central experience of our lives, I too felt myself cut off, before I had even started, from an emerging generation for whom the war was an irrelevance and Britain's imperial past, on which I had been brought up, an obscenity.

I cannot say this sense of alienation and deprivation lasted long but it was devastating while it did. Writers do not quite go in and out of fashion the way that painters do, nor are they so susceptible to prevailing notions about what constitutes an acceptable style, but I learned enough through the dismissal

49

of my earlier literary heroes to sympathize with Keith when a new kind of painting appeared to threaten everything he stood for. In fact, he came to terms with it remarkably quickly and derived something of value from it.

We had a party for the publication of Keith's *Journals and Drawings* at the Redfern Gallery, where John Synge and Harry Tatlock Miller had arranged a small show of his work. By this time Keith had been taken up by what was then called the Marlborough New London Gallery, subsequently Marlborough Fine Art.

For the next fifteen years or so the Marlborough, despite various setbacks, was the most prestigious gallery in London, with a branch in New York. Francis Bacon, Lucian Freud, Graham Sutherland, Henry Moore, Victor Pasmore and Sidney Nolan all showed there. With Keith, for one reason or another, it never really worked out. He had three shows – 1964, 1965 and 1968 – at the Marlborough, after which he came to a happier arrangement with Leslie Waddington, at whose galleries he showed until his death.

The *Journals* were disappointingly received on the whole, being ignored by the daily and Sunday papers and getting only a handful of reviews elsewhere. The book, with over a hundred drawings and photographs, was beautifully printed by the Shenval Press and it is hard to think of any comparable work by an English painter. We could hardly sell a copy at the time but over the years its reputation, and the demand for it, have steadily grown. It has long been unobtainable, and in consequence has become a collector's piece. Interest in it was revived when, six years after Keith's death, I printed in the *London Magazine* three long extracts from the journal he had continued to keep until, literally, the moment of his death.

The published journal was selected from forty-eight notebooks, dating from 1939 to 1965. From 1967 until his death ten years later he filled another thirteen notebooks, most of them orange-covered student's pads with lined pages. What dismayed his friends was the picture these suggested of the miserable existence he thought he was leading while his life appeared to be agreeable, prosperous and successful.

A relaxed, contented journal might make for entertaining reading but it would be unlikely to have the extraordinary effect of these descriptions of a descent into hell. The published volume was of especial interest to students of painting and to anyone curious about the working and thinking habits of a contemporary painter. The extracts from the unpublished journals were less to do with art and more to do with the chronicle of a decline. Keith felt he had worked out ways of dealing with technical problems and after 1970 was just going through the motions.

Most journals tend to reflect on depressed moods and moments and to that extent give an unbalanced picture of the writer's life at any particular time. Keith's are no exception. Mostly they were written late at night when, rather drunk and having failed as usual to make any social arrangement, he found himself alone. He persisted, at much cost to himself, in the belief that social life was scarcely ever worth the candle, that the effort of seeing people, even close friends, far outweighed the rewards. None of this would have mattered if he had enjoyed his solitude, but it was quite plain that he did not. After all, he had been alone the whole day. It was the more misguided in view of the fact that I cannot recall a single evening when, cajoled into coming out, he did not appear to have enjoyed himself.

The routine in Belsize Park over the years covered by the journal rarely varied. He painted, or at any rate was installed, in his studio from about 9.30 to 12.30, after which he had a drink, a snack and a siesta. After tea he worked for another hour or so, read, and then at about seven o'clock had his first whisky. He took trouble over preparing his solitary dinner, chose a bottle of good wine, and, after he had eaten, watched TV. He worked spasmodically at his journal, usually reflecting on the news of the day, on what he was reading, and regretting the lack of human contact and sexual incident in his life. As the number of whiskies increased so did he tend to become obsessively introverted and morbid. The last sentences of the day often petered out into an incoherent scrawl. By the time he was ready for bed and his assortment of pills – anti-depressants, tranquillizers – he was fairly drunk. He may not, on non-teaching days, have spoken a single word all day.

At the time of the first entry to these later journals Keith was fifty-five, had recently been made an Honorary Fellow of the Royal College of Art and been awarded the CBE. He had returned a few months earlier from a visit to North Africa, a journey that resulted in a rich haul of gouaches. He was teaching part-time at the Slade.

It is not surprising, given the lateness of the hour at which it was written and the amount of alcohol Keith consumed, that the journal paints such a one-sided picture of his life. The reason he wrote so little here about his work, Keith himself explained, was because he had been physically involved in it all day. His journal was the record of the left-over part of his life, much of it taken up with discussing food and wine, his tax affairs (which had got him into some trouble) and sexual fantasizing.

In bulk the journals are repetitive and extremely depressing to read, but their frankness, spleen and dry humour, together with the fact that Keith's comments on books and painting are nearly always original and to the point, redeem them. They may be preoccupied with thoughts of failure, illness, suicide and death, of life going by pointlessly, but they are not self-pitying.

Although a natural hypochondriac – he diagnosed the onset

of cancer in himself twenty years before it arrived – Keith had enough real trouble in his last years. He had no sooner recovered from an operation on his kidneys, which had caused him pain for months, than the first real symptoms of cancer appeared. The surgery was not successful and he was faced with further courses of debilitating treatment. The cancer would surely have killed him within a year if he had not got in first.

Despite the wretchedness of all this, it was only in the diary entries of the final eighteen months that the battle was shown to be lost. Never once, either in hospital or convalescing at home after the two operations, did he complain aloud. Whenever I went to see him he was smiling and joking, quite different from the brooding and grumpy creature of Hamilton Terrace mornings thirty years earlier.

Keith's diaries are of unique professional interest, not just for his comments on fellow painters and the art of his time, though these are usually slyly valuable, but also for the insights they provide into the life of a particular kind of contemporary artist, in Keith's case a homosexual. Had he been heterosexual, his life and painting would have been quite different, though whether he would have been any happier or a more fulfilled painter is another matter. He was absolutely what he was and though in his first abstract works the influence of others such as de Stael are recognizable, for the last twenty years of his life no mark that he made or line that he drew could possibly have been made by anyone else. In 1965, in a journal entry roughly dismissive of Julian Maclaren-Ross's view of the '40s, Keith wrote, "They were not like that. For a time there was real life and gaiety. Real things were happening and being done. People were alive. Nothing seemed impossible or too vast to attempt."

People have their moments of optimism at different times and later they remember things differently. I don't think the '40s were a particularly promising period for most of us, and

53

Maclaren-Ross's re-creation of the time, caricature though it is, seems to me to catch its flavour. But while Julian, after a brief period of success, was on the ropes, owing money, and living from hand to mouth at this time, Keith was making his way with a safe job and a growing reputation. One was watching the lights dim, the other was sensing that they would get brighter.

Having grown out of his one attempt at a domestic relationship which he yet felt obliged to honour, Keith spent most of his life in a state of acute sexual frustration. His forays into the homosexual underworld were spectacularly unsuccessful, and such encounters as led to sexual consummation of a sort were rarely repeated. Though quite tough in his dealings with "rough trade" he was often exploited by criminals or near criminals. His diaries are only too explicit about what did or did not go on.

As a last desperate resort he rigged up for himself some kind of masturbatory contrivance that, though depressing to read about and imagine, appeared to give him pleasure. As early as ten years before his death he was observing:

> From the previous Wed, until the Tuesday night the longest and most perfect Karezza ever. Extraordinary buoyancy and zest throughout the day followed by four- to five-hour sessions (electric) each evening. 3 grs Tuinol – perfect sleep – fresh next day. No ill effects after a mild ache in the groin which passed off after 48 hours. I note this simply to record that there is something unique and supremely satisfying in this process as has been repeatedly claimed. Mostly it lies in the sense of self-mastery and superbly controlled pleasure.

The last sentence indicates what must have appealed to Keith's orderly and disciplined nature. The device was not always a success and the causes of failure are as carefully monitored as if he were embarked on experimental orchestral recordings. Conducted as they were over several hours to the accompaniment of wine and music, the sessions were immensely time-consuming, but they provided physical if not emotional release and appeared to have done no damage. They are perhaps sadder for those who were fond of Keith to contemplate than they were in reality. His own typically matter-of-fact comments on surrogate sex have a scientist's detachment.

Writing these words I leaf through the journals at random, and cannot help smiling to myself. Keith's tone of voice comes off every page as if he were standing beside me – his pleasure at certain pieces of music, at male beauty in art, at the boy king Tutankhamen, for instance: "If I had to choose one work from the long history of human artefacts I would choose that gold mask, the onyx eyes, tear-stained gold cheeks." Most of all, though, I hear his voice in the caustic comments that his reading provoked; on Freud's theories about masturbation, for example, or on Maurice Bowra's memoirs: "What a bore. Correct, upper class, and orthodox in everything. No feeling of a real person . . . certainly shan't read it." And on Rothko: "Feeble stuff. Boring to paint and look at. Not surprising he killed himself if that was all there was to do." There are also typically painterly observations: "White light and silence everywhere. Harvest moon. A bigness which wipes out all small things. The white corn against white sky. No sound. Absolute purity and stillness. Two silent bats. I hate to turn on the light to write this." Some of his reflections make me laugh out loud: "What was Rimbaud's cock like? What a pity such things are completely undocumented (I'm not interested in Verlaine's. He shouldn't have one)." I can hear Keith saying this last sentence brusquely and then giggling. For all the melancholy implications of the journals they provide evidence in every entry of love of life, love of beauty, love of humanity, hatred of injustice, hatred of falseness, hatred of hypocrisy.

Once what Keith called 'the Cancer Era' had begun, he prepared for death. He claimed that it did not worry him but that he wanted to make a graceful exit. "Not in pain or prostration. And alone, alas, because I can see how good it would be to die holding someone's hand. But I do not know anyone to whom this would be agreeable." He was wrong in this, of course, but it was a part of his reluctance to make demands on his friends. "Decision-making nearly always induces panic," he wrote. "A very limited field of choice suits me better than wide horizons of opportunity. I claim no merit in this timid attitude to life, but I never acquired the weapons of a warrior. I have something of the shrewdness and cunning of small mammals."

In the hot summer and early autumn of 1977 Keith was often in pain, as well as suffering from radiation sickness, and he brooded daily on the best methods of suicide, on the questions of how and when. The idea of a ceremonial suicide in the presence of close friends appealed to him. "As I got dozy I would take my leave of being, one by one, with sadness but not despair. And not lonely. It would be a ritualized affair, civilized and well conducted."

It was not like that in the event. Yet the last entry, so evocative of character and of Keith's attachment to truth, is not really sad either:

> 4 November 9.30 a.m. The capsules have been taken
> with some whisky. What is striking is the unreality of
> the situation. I feel no different . . . But suddenly the
> decision came that it must be done. I cannot drag on
> another few years in this state. It's a bright sunny
> morning. Full of life. Such a morning as many people
> have died on. I am ready for death though I fear it. Of
> course the whole thing may not work and I shall wake
> up. I don't really mind either way. Once the decision
> seemed inevitable the courage needed was less than I

thought. I don't quite believe anything has happened though the bottle is empty. At the moment I feel very much alive ... I cannot believe I have committed suicide since nothing has happened. No big bang or cut wrists. 65 was long enough for me. It wasn't a complete failure I did some. ...

At this point the writing lapsed into illegibility and ran down and off the page.

The cremation at Golders Green, on a cold, blustery day, was about as gloomy an affair as could be. A few friends huddled in coats – Patrick Procktor, Leonard Rosoman, John Synge among them, and Ramsay in a state of collapse, propped up as if he were a sandbag – and then out into the rain. It was bleakly in keeping, as if Keith himself had washed his hands of it.

In thirty years, except for brief holidays, he had rarely left North London, moving a few miles only, from Hamilton Terrace to Belsize Park. In those years the art of his time had altered out of all recognition. Through all changes he remained dourly observant but unaffected, an unwillingly heroic figure. He had outlived Johnny by nearly twenty years. Neither had been among my closest friends during the time I had known them but they had educated me in the ways of painting and they had been, in their different ways, generous and welcoming when I had nowhere to live and few ideas about what to do. Their pictures, on the walls of the room in which I write, mean, as a consequence, more to me than any others.

Iowa and Keith Vaughan

Learning of your suicide,
The customary calm of your ending
In that methodical way,
The remorseless advance of the enemy
You could not stop gaining on you,

I look up
At your paintings of Iowa,
Cedar Rapids, Des Moines, Omaha,
Remembering my own journeys
Through that unpopulated landscape
West of Chicago – unpopulated
Because she wasn't with me – my notes

So similar to those scratched
In the margins of your drawings,
As if it were them
I travelled through,
Not the real thing, that emptiness
Spilling its way to the Pacific.

You observed:
"Red oxide barns with silver pinnacles"
"Pink pigs bursting from black earth like truffles"
"Ochre sticks of corn stubble"
"Space and sun"

And approaching Omaha
"For sale – Night Crawlers"
"The air of expectation; of probing contacts"
"Extraordinary prevalence of mortuaries,
Neon-lit and glittering like cinemas".

What you drew
Were the black barns and white-timbered houses
Reminding you of Essex,
Snow patches and corn stooks,

Silos erect on the countryside like penises,
The starched white
Fences protective of loneliness.

I am in Iowa again,
Landlocked and frozen
In a numbing death of the spirit –
You knew before your own
How many forms death takes.

Death of a Fly

Raising my pen to put a point
On the page, a dot over an i,
An unsteadily veering fly
Collides in a three-point landing, and settles.
Then, as if carving a joint,
It carefully sharpens its legs,
Sitting up the way a dog begs.
I notice a wing shed like a petal.
It has come here to die.
And my dot, streaked now with blood,
Turns the colour of mud.

Romantics

When the time comes
They will give up home,
Children, days of long
Memory, for that song

Conjured out of air,
Which draws from its lair
The most reclusive beast,
Who answers to it least.

Limits

It could never be.
This, they knew,
As also, could it,
Would grow less true.

To weigh against this,
Set their each kiss,
Perfectly circumscribed,
Exactly what it is.

A Card from the Café Pierre Loti

High over the Horn
Mosques and factories spectral on water
The same tables set among pines
The same sunsets reviving as alcohol
The smell of charcoal and mint tea
And towards Izmir the same steamers
Bringing the East nearer

Which already inhabited him,
This Turk by adoption, in high collar
And tarboosh, moustaches askew,
Luckier than most of us
To have acquired so exotic a view

From his own fantasies, reclining among silk
Cushions, hookah at his elbow.

You can see him happily
Dolled up on the back of this postcard,
Host to an evening of imperial twilight.
His books no longer read, the dark
Falls on him, as on this muddle
Of domes and smokestacks, the East's
Voluptuous visions reduced to images
Of penury. Still, the pages
Have a curious scent, improbably haunting.

On the Bosphorus

Below my balcony a swarthy contralto,
Her face like a sweetmeat,
All hair and secret emulsions,
Soaps at her bosom. She juggles it,
Warbling *Aida*. Often at night
I watch her embracing the moon
Shuffling her roof in see-through nightdress.

She distracts me, as now
Do two teams of birds, come upon
One another as if by chance,
Who toss her drawers as they dry
In some kind of aerial tennis,
Worrying the mauve satin
With the same exaggerated persistence dogs
And lawyers affect when odours resist them.

PART II

With Morgan to Baghdad

NOT LONG AFTER Johnny Minton and I returned from Corsica I received my summons from the British Council. But first I went twice to Hamburg, as if drawn back there by a mixture of nostalgia and curiosity, by the feeling that there was something I had not done.

A civilian now, I called in on old haunts like the Atlantic Bar. I had only been gone a year but the personnel looked older, fatter and up to their ears in the Black Market. The war trials were still going on in almost deserted courtrooms, an insignificant little man in a crumpled green uniform being meticulously questioned about how he had spent the afternoon of 8 May 1942 in Sachsenhausen. The thoroughness and careful sifting of evidence was admirable, but so long after the end of the war it held little interest. Because of the necessity to translate everything, the simplest exchange of information – "How many Allied nationals were in the camp on the day the witness alleges he saw you strike the deceased?" – took an age. The impartiality of this dispensation of justice remained impressive. People drifted in and out of the court, whose doors were open to whoever wished to enter, but the events it dealt with were already impossibly remote.

Rebuilding had started but the floating population of many thousands wandered in a kind of perpetual sleepwalk from underground to bunker to railway station. No refugee was allowed officially to stay in Hamburg for more than three days, yet in the network of passages under the Hauptbahnhof a whole ghost city had grown up, impossible to shift. Totally apathetic and sunken-eyed, half-starved, these were people with nowhere to go, prisoners of their own past. It was as if the imagination had erected its own bars, shutting them in. They came to life only when the free meals – stew and black bread – were trundled around. Then, blinking like moles, they emerged briefly into the light, aimlessly circling the rubble, anxious only that their square yard of sanctuary had not been seized in their absence. So it would be for another year. After that the nightmare would be over.

It was not all gloom. Posters on the stumps of columns announced plays by Anouilh, Giraudoux, Brecht, Hausmann and Tagore. Britten's *Peter Grimes* was due shortly. The firm of Rowohlt was bringing out paperback translations of Graham Greene, Christopher Isherwood, Sartre, Hemingway and Saint-Exupéry in editions of 100,000 copies each. Best of all, the nauseating smell of buried bodies that used to float over from Harburg and hang over the city had gone.

I made a pilgrimage to the docks, the scene once of such frenzied activity, and where I had spent so much time. The great shipyards of Bloem & Voss were now silent, the green curve of the Elbe scarcely broken by any bow wave. At Pier 47 groups of sailors hung about, hoping for ships that would never come.

The beating heart of the port had stopped, and only a minesweeping flotilla, based at Cuxhaven, was still working. Yet at night St Pauli still miraculously came to life, an amorphous crowd of refugees, sailors, ex-servicemen spilling out of dance halls and cabarets, or wandering through Herbert Strasse where, in their brightly-lit rooms, the familiar whores in their regulation black stockings and suspender belts tapped on the windows with their fans to attract attention.

66

It was not much of a spectacle, and there was not much money to be thrown around, but it was something. In what seemed later like no time at all, such was the speed of the German recovery, a gleaming new-old city had been re-assembled out of concrete and glass. There was no longer anything to try to come to terms with or need to expiate.

Before office life closed in on me, I wrote about all this in the pages of *Tribune* and the *Spectator*; infant efforts from my early days as a journalist. James Pope-Hennessy was briefly literary editor of the latter, and at *Tribune* Tosco Fyvel, with whose successor Bruce Bain (later metamorphosed into Richard Findlater) I also worked, was an encouraging mentor. Alan Pryce-Jones had recently taken over as editor of *The Times Literary Supplement*, and before the end of the year I had been allowed to indulge my interest in Saint-Exupéry, James Hanley and Ernst Jünger, and to review books by Auden and Keith Douglas. With occasional broadcasts on the Third Programme and several poems laconically accepted by Joe Ackerley for the *Listener*, it was a start. None of the criticism seems to me now particularly penetrating or well argued, but I was interested in what I was doing and I was re-educating myself as I went along.

I had scarcely got settled into my British Council work in Grosvenor Square when I was sent for by the Controller of Education, Arthur Morgan, who asked if I would like to accompany him as his personal assistant on a trip to Iraq. Arthur Morgan had, it turned out, been on the Rockefeller Atlantic Awards committee that had given me money the year before. He reminded me of the story I had sent in, amazing me by his recall of its erotic detail and by his obvious pleasure in it.

Arthur Morgan was in his early sixties at the time, a tall, grey-haired man with a manner that varied between the parsonical, the fussily irritable and the genially mischievous. Born in the West Country, he had been a university lecturer, a civil servant, and Principal of both University College, Hull and McGill University, Montreal. Before joining the British Council, he had been an Assistant Secretary at the Ministry of Labour and National Service.

Arthur was one of those immensely well-organized men for whom committees seem to exist. He was a big shot in the Council with radical ideas about the teaching of English and the reorganization of the Council's educational policy. What Arthur liked to do was to draft out a paper and then fly round the world at the Government's expense discussing it. His ability to transform high-powered work into pleasure was an enviable quality but his high-handed methods and assumption of total freedom to do what he liked and go where he pleased eventually got him into disrepute. He was, however, an interesting man, knowledgeable on a wide range of subjects, and he was generous and kind to me.

It appeared that the Iraqis were proposing to found a new university at Baghdad, and Morgan, consulted at some early stage, was anxious that it should be developed on British rather than French lines. The French were apparently keen to establish an interest but Morgan had got in first, proposing a two-man mission, consisting of himself and Sir Charles Darwin, an eminent Cambridge scientist and grandson of the great naturalist and author of *On the Origin of Species*. Morgan, a natural private empire-builder, offered me the post of secretary to the mission.

Naturally I was delighted at the chance of free travel, but since I had no secretarial skills and could not even type I expressed reservations about my suitability. Morgan brushed these aside. It soon became clear that what he wanted was a vaguely presentable ADC who would provide alternative company to Sir Charles, a bluff, unworldly specialist whose range of interests might not coincide with Arthur's own. Also, the Iraqis were paying for the expedition and it would obviously be more impressive if the two eminent educationists had someone to do any dogsbodying that might be necessary. The Director of my department at the British Council, a large, rather meringue-like lady of benevolent but commanding appearance, was not keen on such blatant poaching of her junior staff but Morgan's word was law and her objections were soon overruled.

We flew via Rome, lunching at the palatial British Council quarters with Ronald Bottrall, the Representative. The Council in Rome was very grand in those days and Ronald Bottrall was a man of similar stamp to Morgan, at least in his style of living and assumption of proconsular behaviour. Bottrall, whose reputation as a poet had suffered from F. R. Leavis's aggressive advocacy, served in many capacities and countries and it was unlikely that the Council was undervalued in any of the capitals that he graced. But whereas Bottrall was something of a cultural elitist, Morgan held more populist views. It was his conviction that the sources of future influence, both cultural and political, lay in spreading the gospel of the English language. Although a scholar, he was by nature a social reformer and his ideas on education would have been well suited to the Arts Council during the time of Roy Shaw.

My own interest in the British Council as a possible career had been influenced by its standing abroad and by friends, mostly writers, who worked for it, either before or more or less at the same time as myself: Louis MacNeice and Rex Warner in Greece, for example; Bernard Spencer in Cairo, and later Madrid and Vienna, Francis King and Frank Tuohy variously in Japan, Poland and South America. I had in mind cultural ambassadors such as George Seferis, Octavio Paz, Pablo Neruda and Leopold Senghor, poets I admired and who were employed as diplomats, and I was thinking of the way in which the French and various other European countries habitually made use of their best writers.

Ideally, the British Council seemed to offer the best of all worlds to someone like myself, but, whether or not directly as a result of Arthur Morgan's policies, there was, within a decade, scarcely a writer left on its staff. The emphasis veered steadily away from the arts towards science and education, and in the process a different type of person came to be recruited. As a result the prestige of the Council as a cultural institution undoubtedly declined, though perhaps there were benefits of a more practical kind.

At the time, Beaverbrook was carrying on such a vindictive vendetta against the Council and all its activities that it was difficult even to get secretarial staff. The general public was being given the impression in article after article that the Council, if not treasonable, was farcical – probably both – and consisted entirely of homosexuals. This was far from the truth, but a climate was created in which defensive attitudes developed and made it easier for someone like Arthur Morgan to carry out sweeping changes.

Between Rome and Baghdad I found myself sitting next to Agatha Christie, noticing her quiet assurance and fat legs. Her husband, the archaeologist Max Mallowan, was, for some reason, in the row behind. Every year she accompanied him on one of his digs, most of which were in either Syria or Iraq. Max Mallowan seemed much in the shadow, physically and temperamentally, of his larger and older wife, whom he had married when he was only twenty-six and she already a famous writer. Max had been a member of the British Museum Expedition to Nineveh before the war and I think they were on their way there now, prior to Max taking over the Directorship of the British School of Archaeology in Iraq, a post he held for the next fifteen years. At the Embassy in Baghdad I looked them both up in *Who's Who*. Agatha sensibly did not give her age, but I learned that her hobby was bathing and Max's was trees, which conjured up pastoral scenes of Agatha, in a clinging costume, cavorting like a hippo in the shallows of some winding river, while Max stretched out on the bank, re-creating prehistoric Assyria or recalling youthful frolics in the Balikh Valley. I was to see a good deal of them both in the weeks to come. Agatha told me on the plane that she preferred reading poetry to anything else. Back in England I sent her a copy of my first book but since she failed to acknowledge it I presumed she hadn't cared for it. I didn't myself much either.

Shortly after her return Agatha set a murder story in Iraq, called, rather prosaically for her, *They Came to Baghdad*. I thought at one stage of the trip that she was going to have material for a plot rather earlier than she could have anticipated. On a short flight into the desert to look at some ruins a week after our arrival, I was sitting next to Arthur Morgan, who was busy preparing a memorandum, his favourite activity. My main task was to circulate these at meetings with Iraqi politicians and university officials, and often I had the impression that the endless draftings of minutes and agenda were made simply to justify my presence.

I was gazing out of the window of our light plane when I became aware that Morgan was muttering beside me. He had gone red in the face and was repeating, "That man's looking at me. I don't like the way he's looking at me." I looked up and there, a row or two in front, was an apparently respectable middle-aged Iraqi half-turned in his seat. It was difficult to assess whether Morgan's muttering had attracted his attention or whether he actually had been showing an unseemly curiosity in Morgan's papers. When this man caught my gaze he held it quite coolly, continuing to cast an inquisitive, though not particularly obtrusive eye at Morgan. He seemed no more than a habitual starer, of a kind common enough in the Middle East and elsewhere.

Whatever the reason for his behaviour, it was too much for Morgan. Before I could restrain him he had flung his papers down, risen to his feet and demanded of the surprised fellow:

"What's the matter with you, do you want some glasses to read my notes, is that what you want?" Whereupon he strode forward and began shaking the man by the collar. Taken aback, the victim of this sudden assault also got to his feet and for a few seconds they confronted each other in the aisle, Arthur scarlet and sweating, the other man plainly rattled, his eyes darting from side to side as if seeking escape.

I caught Agatha's eye in the row behind but it was evident she was relishing the spectacle. The Iraqi, attempting to recover his composure, gave Arthur a push, enough to send him off balance and deposit him in the nearest seat. The plane now began to bank steeply and further recriminations would have had to be conducted at a very odd angle indeed. The pilot's voice crackled over the intercom, pointing out the pipeline glinting beneath us and the oases of Jumat Qa Qa'ara and Qasr Amij to port and starboard.

By the time we were back on an even keel the stuffing had gone out of Arthur, though he continued to mutter unintelligibly until we arrived back at Baghdad. The Iraqi, now that the danger was over, adopted a more hostile air, repeatedly brushing his suit down and straightening his tie, and addressed the other passengers in Arabic, presumably on the inconvenience of travelling with a lunatic. Arthur had a genuine streak of paranoia which on occasion boiled over like a car radiator; afterwards he would gradually settle down and chuckle as though nothing had happened. To my amazement I saw him clutch the Iraqi's arm as we were disembarking, starting up a conversation as if they were old friends. The man recoiled but then, thinking it better to humour a mad Englishman, suffered himself to be led across the tarmac by an Arthur now in full spate and as merry as a grig.

The incident had reminded me of my old friend of Soho days, the painter Gerald Wilde, whose own paranoia was generally directed at the police. We would be walking along talking when Gerald would suddenly halt in his tracks, eyes popping. "How dare he look at me like that!" he would demand, gesturing at a policeman on point duty who was quite oblivious to Gerald's presence. "How dare he? This is not a police state." It would be only with the greatest difficulty that one could prevent Gerald from rushing through the traffic and accosting the innocent officer. With his mad eyes and long flapping overcoat Gerald, at other times the gentlest creature imaginable, would have been an unnerving sight.

Our arrival in Baghdad was not quite as anticipated. During the last lap of the flight there had been an attempted coup against the Iraqi government, and instead of being welcomed with garlands we found ourselves being escorted off the plane by armed guards. There was the sound of gunfire in the distance and a notable display of tanks and other armoured vehicles on the airfield perimeter.

None of this was to Arthur's liking, and his petulant manner seemed to indicate that the inconvenience was personally directed at him. He waved dismissively at the various paraphernalia, as though to suggest that these were toys being played with by children. A bullet whistling past his ear moderated his grumbling and he was soon mollified by the appearance of several high-ranking officials, profuse in their apologies. We departed in a convoy of limousines with darkened windows, preceded and followed by a motorcycle escort.

Charles Darwin was one of those self-contained, unsurprised and enquiring men in whose eyes nothing that happens is extraordinary. He regarded Arthur's volatile behaviour and Middle East political intrigue with the same scientific detachment, barely appearing to notice that anything untoward was taking place. Immensely informed on what seemed to me every subject under the sun, he carried on a polite discourse with whoever was at hand. Nothing appeared to put him out in any way. This was just as well, for no sooner were we installed in the Tigris Palace, which itself was sandbagged and guarded by troops, than a curfew was imposed on the city. For several days none of us could go out. From time to time meetings were held in our suite, but the discussions seemed unreal in the circumstances and our visitors nervous.

While Sir Charles appeared to look on our incarceration as an act of God, busying himself meanwhile with various scientific papers he had brought with him, Arthur grew more and more agitated. This was not his idea of fun. One of his most engaging characteristics was his assumption that hard work and a good time should not be mutually exclusive. To this end he bent his endeavours unremittingly. He had come to Baghdad to implement a carefully considered and elaborately worked-out scheme, of equal future benefit to Iraq and to Britain, but he had also come to see something of the country. Only the frequent disturbances in the streets adjoining the hotel and occasional attacks on the hotel itself, resulting in broken windows, restrained him from private acts of folly. He took the view that the whole business was a lot of nonsense and that any differences of opinion between the various parties could be settled in a morning by someone like himself. He was probably right, for when not crossed in his private demands Arthur was sweet reasonableness itself.

In spite of the situation, we did, in fact, make some progress. Government emissaries, university administrators, architects, academics continued to call, singly or to attend meetings, the academics anxious to establish departmental rights in lecture halls or laboratories. I would take notes and in the evening arrange for them to be typed up, incorporating Sir Charles's observations and Arthur's proposals.

In due course the siege was lifted and we were free to come and go. I had never been anywhere near the Middle East before and the only cities I could compare to Baghdad were Bombay and Calcutta. But while the Tigris, when at last I was able to hire a boat and sail on it, reminded me of the Hooghly, the sun turning the water copper-coloured, there was little of the noise and bustle of an Indian city here. In

Calcutta the banks of the Hooghly are public places, with bathing ghats leading off promenades, and the maidan and the Botanical Gardens with their huge banyan trees running flush with the river. In Baghdad much of the western bank seemed to consist of private houses, built in the Turkish style around courtyards and with river frontages of their own.

There is nothing like the Hooghly Bridge, with its clutter of bullock carts, rickshaws, cows, trucks and buses, to arrest the eye on the Tigris. The three bridges that cross the river are comparatively puny and whenever I went sailing, usually in the early morning or evening, I had the feeling that Baghdad, despite its antiquity and sudden accretion of wealth, was a temporary affair that might disappear overnight. It was the river that was permanent, holding the place together, moving supplies and stores, feeding the countryside.

Although hideous buildings were going up on all sides, just as many were coming down, and there seemed no distinct division between town and country. Many of the older buildings were of mud and thatch and when it rained the whole place looked in danger of melting and slithering into the river. At dawn, with the river still and flat as a sword blade, and again at dusk, with the sun flushing the trunks of the date palms, it seemed miraculously beautiful but half-rural.

This was not the impression we were meant to carry away. With Iraq's sudden wealth from oil, the idea was that Baghdad was an expanding modern city about to become an oriental metropolis. We were only there because of this sophisticated vision, which incorporated modern hospitals, housing estates, palatial government buildings, hotels and new universities. Indeed there was evidence all round of such schemes being implemented. Yet I could never rid myself of a sense of impermanence, of the idea that the oil would suddenly dry up and Baghdad sink back into the desert with it.

Arthur began to worry that I wasn't enjoying myself enough, that though I went sailing and played squash at the club nearly every day, I was too much with old people. He thought I should get out on my own more, and not have to dine just with him and Sir Charles in the gloomy Tigris Palace dining-room. I told him not to be concerned, and in any case there weren't any young people, at least not any with whom I could communicate.

One morning he tapped on my bedroom door, his eyes gleaming with excitement. On his evening walk in Rashid Street the night before he had been accosted by a negro, one of the numerous youths that prowled the city streets. Baghdad, like most capitals of the East, suffered a daily influx of bored adolescents for whom their adopted countryside held few attractions. They arrived in the city, failed to find work, and so were obliged to scrounge as best they could, living off their bodies, pimping, or touting for shopkeepers.

Arthur had already shown a lively interest in the brothel quarters, though his concern was, I think, sociological and voyeuristic rather than practical. His acquaintance of the night before, whom he called Lofty, had accompanied him back to the hotel, promising all kinds of delights. I could imagine Arthur's eyes glinting keenly through his spectacles, his sexual and anthropological curiosity equally aroused. All his life he had been involved in social work, much of it to do with boys' clubs in depressed areas, and I began to envisage a Gladstone-like situation arising. Lofty, it appeared, was going to look out for us the next night.

Arthur chortled away over breakfast, which we usually shared, since we had connecting rooms. It was enough for him to enjoy vicarious fantasies but I had a feeling that Lofty, once encountered, would not easily be shaken off. Arthur, though concerned that Sir Charles might observe him being greeted by Lofty as if he were an old friend, thought it quite reasonable for me to bear that burden. Lofty had intimated to Arthur that he had at his disposal the choicest specimens of both sexes; virgins, naturally, and handpicked by Lofty himself for a local sheikh. Their availability to Arthur and his friend was a little business he was conducting on the side.

It became impossible over the next few days to leave the hotel without Lofty emerging from some hidden vantage point and implanting himself beside us. Each time he appeared in a different rig, usually a dilapidated three-piece suit, no socks and thick-soled shoes. Sometimes he was simply dressed in the white or striped knee-length garment known as a dish-dasha, occasionally with his suit jacket over it, and on one memorable occasion he sported an ankle-length wrap-around skirt under which a suede shoe protruded on one foot and a dirty gym shoe on the other. His headgear was less various, being generally a skullcap topped by a loosely tied headcloth of the sort coolies wear in the Calcutta docks. Once he appeared in a rakish fedora, which made me laugh. This hurt his feelings and he never wore it again, though I assured him he looked very elegant; it was just that he had taken me by surprise.

Since we tended to be accompanied out of the hotel by respectable university dignitaries, Arthur began to regret his earlier encouragement of Lofty and would wave him away. This did not deter Lofty but he tended now to transfer attention to me. We would set off in a group, Arthur and Sir Charles ahead, with official escorts, Lofty and I in the rear.

I began to miss Lofty on the rare occasions when he failed to turn up, since he always had some gossip of political or erotic interest. He would answer my questions about his family and his religious practices with patience, encouraging me to visit the marshes which was where he came from. Perhaps I would hire a boat and we could go together?

Before this could happen I succumbed one evening to Lofty's entreaties. It was very bad for his reputation, he suggested, that no result was coming from all the meetings he was having with us. His various contacts were getting suspicious, each imagining he was doing business with another or that he was operating on his own behalf. So, on a night when Arthur and

77

Sir Charles were involved with university affairs that did not need my presence, I decided to put Lofty to the test. Surprise me, I said, let us see all these wonderful creatures you have at your disposal.

He was less delighted to be taken at his word than I had expected. He began to waggle his head about, saying yes yes, I will show you wonderful time, but these things must be arranged. He would contact me again when he had fixed it up. I had been under the impression that we would set off there and then, but it became plain that Lofty was very low down on the procuring ladder and that, far from having a harem at his fingertips, he himself now had to make enquiries. I was not interested enough to hang about and told Lofty it was now or never. No, no, he said, it was no problem, but he wouldn't want me to be disappointed by getting just any girl. He would be in touch next day.

It so happened that we were going to be out of Baghdad for a few days so I imagined that would be the end of the matter. But the evening of our return Lofty was waiting.

Everything was arranged, he said, what time would I like to set off? My curiosity about Lofty's entrepreneurial talents had declined during our absence and I made various excuses. But he looked so unbelievably stricken that his great efforts on my behalf, made in all good faith, should come to nothing, with consequent loss of face on his part, that I allowed myself to be persuaded. I agreed to meet him after dinner.

Lofty was wearing what I used to call his ponce's suit, its three-piece effect spoiled by his lack of tie and his stubble. We set off across Rashid Street and down a series of side streets and alleyways. After about twenty minutes, by which time we had entered a kind of kasbah sealed off by mud walls, I began to get restless and wanted to go back. Only another few yards, Lofty said, nearly there.

We may have been nearly there but it soon became clear Lofty had lost his way. He darted up and down narrow maze-like streets, often ones we had passed through earlier. There was scarcely anyone about, though Arab music drifted from courtyards behind padlocked doors and smells of scent and cooking mingled with those of flowers, beer and dung. Motioning me to wait for him, Lofty, sweating profusely, now shot off on his own. I had no idea where we were and no confidence that I should ever find my way out should I wish to try. Every so often a muffled figure sidled past me and it needed no great act of imagination for me to envisage being robbed or having my throat cut.

At last Lofty returned, and it was obvious from his expression that whatever arrangements he had made had fallen through. He was not apologetic but balefully silent and surly. Now he had lost face with me.

Eventually we found ourselves back at the Tigris Palace. Lofty cheered up. Tomorrow, he said, I get much better girl, these ones no good, not honourable families. But tomorrow I was going to Basra. Lofty was crestfallen. Arthur Morgan was very disappointed at the outcome of the evening.

One night in the bar of the Tigris Palace I met an old friend from my Fleet Air Arm days. Hugh had flown Swordfish and Walruses, at a time when we had nothing else to fly, from the air station at Lee-on-Solent, HMS *Daedalus*, scene of my farcical but perilous encounter with the Commander (Flying). That, as described in *Blindfold Games*, had almost ended in disaster. After I had left Lee-on-Solent, hauled out for a German code interception course before joining HMS *Onslow*, Hugh had gone on to become a very distinguished pilot indeed, one of the few of my colleagues of those days to survive. We had kept vaguely in touch.

He was now attached to the Sheikh of Kuwait as his private pilot. He was going back there in a few days' time and suggested I fly with him. The Sheikh was a generous host and always pleased to see visitors. Hugh, in any case, had his own quarters and plenty of room. We agreed on a timetable and Arthur gave me permission, though my three days' leave would have to come out of my annual Council allowance.

Meanwhile an official shooting trip, instigated by the Iraqi Foreign Office, had been arranged for Sir Charles, Arthur and myself. We were to take the train for Basra and there be met by a legendary figure known as the Mighty Hunter. We would then proceed by boat into the marsh country north of the Hammar and Sarraf lakes, where we would study birdlife and the habits of the marsh villagers, and enjoy the hospitality of local sheikhs in their *mudhifs*, guest houses similar to dak bungalows in India; only in this instance it would be a reed-built extension, constructed on the banks of a lagoon, to the sheikh's own stone house. The sheikhs for the most part had African servants and it was from this background that Lofty had sprung.

In the event Sir Charles and Arthur were prevented from coming, and the Mighty Hunter announced that he was indisposed. So I set off for Basra on my own, an "Assistant" Mighty Hunter having been allotted to me, taking the Basra Express.

The main marshes begin west of Al Qurna, where the Euphrates and the Tigris meet and form the Shatt al Arab. The Assistant MH was waiting at Basra station, a spare, military-looking man with a neat moustache. He could, in his crisp khaki shirt and trousers, have been mistaken at first glance for a soldier, the adjutant of a good regiment, except that he was wearing sandals and had no hat. Moreover, his hair was of a more unruly nature than is usually associated with an officers' mess.

He introduced himself formally as the Assistant Mighty Hunter, smiling openly, but not at his title, which seemed to be as gazetted. He apologized for his superior's absence, assuring me that it was because of some gastric disturbance and in no way due to the downgrading of our expedition.

We were soon on our way, a jeep whisking us through the leafy suburbs – a more compact, greener version of Baghdad with clumps of mimosa flowering in riverside gardens – and out into the country. Palm trees stood up against the horizon in all directions, each line of them marking the waterways. The Assistant MH had a bad cold and I was reminded of Gertrude Bell's observation in one of her letters, in the one-volume Benn edition which I had brought with me, about the treachery of the Iraqi climate. "The winter isn't really very nice here. One is usually sneezing when not coughing." Gertrude Bell spent Christmas 1916 in the Basra area and the rain was so insistent that she felt obliged to send to London for an umbrella. It seemed an odd request to have to make, because almost everyone I now saw was equipped with an umbrella, often carried on the shoulder like a rifle, even when riding a bicycle. "Presently I shall have to ask you to send me a nice wig," she wrote to her father. "I haven't got enough hair left to pin a hat to. I don't know what happens to one's hair in this climate. It just evaporates." The Iraqi answer to the problem seemed to be to reduce the hair to a stubble, at least among the humbler classes.

Our boat, a glorified punt, was almost hidden from sight by the tall, golden reeds that rise like porcupine quills on each bank of the narrow channels. The Shatt al Arab spun away to our right, the land so flat that the horizon's curve made us seem to be at the centre of a circle. Downriver we had passed dhows and cargo vessels, but now we were off on some western tributary where the boats, either canoes or rafts, were moved along by paddles or veered under sails the colour of the small clouds that dispersed as the sun climbed.

The few days I spent in the marshes were a kind of dream, coloured the green of reeds, the blondness of corn, the gunmetal shimmer of water, the pale bronze of sky. The noises were the soft splash of poles edging us forward, the plopping of frogs, the honking of geese, and at night, after we had tied up, the remorseless barking of dogs and the sighing of reeds.

For hours at a time we were able to see only the sky directly above us, the reeds forming screens which were sometimes so close together that we would have to push our way through them. We would emerge into open water, the banks backing away, and there, ahead of us, were small villages of reed houses clustered on the edge of infinite plains.

Some years later I used to meet Gavin Maxwell at the house of our mutual friend Patrick Kinross. Gavin's book *A Reed Shaken by the Wind*, an account of his time in the marshes with Wilfred Thesiger, had not yet appeared, though he was writing it. I was surprised when we talked about our experiences to learn that he, like Gertrude Bell, had suffered from appalling weather, because the days and nights I spent there were flawless. Yet day after day Gavin and Thesiger in their *tarada*, a high-prowed craft of more aristocratic lineage than our own, were rained on, buffeted by gales and spun about by sudden gusts that threatened to capsize them. I experienced nothing of the kind.

Of one such day Gavin wrote:

> It was blowing hard and cold when we left the village, the sky was empty and grey without individual clouds . . . The earth seemed flat as a plate and stretched away for ever before us, vast, desolate and pallid . . . As the gusts grew stronger and ruffled the water among the reeds into flurries of small ripples, it tore a chorus of strange sounds from the stiff, withered sedge stumps, groans and whistles, bleats and croaks, and loud crude sounds of flatulence . . . There was no colour anywhere, and the grey sky, unbroken by hill or tree, seemed as immense as from a small boat far out at sea. Occasionally a flight of pelicans would sail majestically by, riding the wind on stiff outstretched wings, rigid and

82

bulky in body as seaplanes; and once a flock of white ibis drifted past very high up, to fan out into a wheeling kaleidoscope of white petals on the great empty sky. It was in some way a terrible landscape, utterly without human sympathy, more desolate and inimical than the sea itself . . . there seemed no refuge for any creature whose blood was warm.

Luckily for me, such days never materialized, nor was I aware of the possibility. I had taken Gertrude Bell as gospel:

I don't know why it should be as attractive as it is. The elements of the scene are extremely simple, but the combination still makes a wonderfully attractive result. Yet there's really nothing – flat, far-stretching plain coming down to the river's edge, thorn-covered, water-covered in the flood in the lower reaches, a little wheat and millet stubble in the base fields, an occasional village of reed-built houses and the beautiful river craft, majestic on noble sails or skimming on clumsy paddles. The river bends and winds, comes back on itself almost and you have the curious apparition of a fleet of white sails rising out of the thorny waste, now on one side of you, now the other.

Before my visit, this area was significant in my mind for the sole reason that my only photograph of my father as an officer has him standing, topi in hand, on a Mesopotamian river bank. On the back of the photograph is written, "Near Basra, 1919".

I had no dramas on the marshes, and my memory of them is as of a mirror on which are embossed clouds, palms, boats and magical sunsets. Gavin wrote of the nights descending in utter desolation, without a hint of colour: "The light just faded out of that roaring grey sky until the silhouettes of the tossing palm plumes became dim and indistinct and merged into the darkness of a starless sky." But he also recorded, when the clouds lifted, colours that had

> the brilliance and clarity of fine enamel. Here in the shelter of the lagoons the reeds, golden as farmyard straw in the sunshine, towered out of water that was beetle-wing blue in the lee of the islands or ruffled where the wind found passage between them to the dull deep green of an uncut emerald. It was a landscape as weird as a Lost World, and through it flew birds as strange and unfamiliar in flight as pterodactyls: snake-necked African darters, pygmy cormorants, pelicans and halcyon kingfishers.

Gavin's book, as well as being a fascinating report on Thesiger at work, doctoring the marsh people, is rich in the kind of animal and bird descriptions at which he became so good. Before inviting himself to Iraq with Thesiger, having come across a 1954 article by the latter, "The Marshmen of Southern Iraq", in the *Journal of the Royal Geographical Society*, Gavin had spent several years in Sicily. He had written two highly successful books about aspects of Sicilian life, as well as *Harpoon at a Venture*, and Iraq, from Thesiger's article, seemed to offer just what he was looking for: the chance to study the life of a primitive and unexplored people before the untamed places became, in Thesiger's words, "suburbanized" and the tribesmen were turned into "corner boys".

At the end of their few weeks together – their trip took place in 1957, ten years after my own visit – Thesiger made Gavin the present of an otter: "He raised to me a blunt face with a black-button nose like a koala bear." He was called Mijbil and he changed Gavin's life, sadly little though there proved to be left of it.

For one reason in particular I am glad to have got to Iraq before Gavin. Had I read *A Reed Shaken by the Wind* befor setting out for the marshes I would have spent my days less serenely, or perhaps not gone at all. As we slipped along between flooded rice fields, with the Assistant MH discoursing on whatever came into view – naked fishermen straining the river through their nets, the water glistening like fish scales, wild pigs cavorting in the undergrowth or swimming across a channel, ibis and duck taking off with startling rattles from almost under our boat, water buffalo dozing in the shallows – I had no idea that the channels in which I often paddled my hands so idly were full of water snakes. My distaste for any kind of snake, harmless or not, makes me reluctant to go knowingly where I might come upon one, and these snakes of the marshes, *arbids*, are, according to Gavin, not only often huge but deadly. The Arabs will not even touch a dead one. In his book he described several encounters with snakes, one of which made my blood run cold. The boat was being paddled through a narrow waterway with tall reeds pressing close on either side. Gavin, happening to look up and catch Thesiger's eye, was astounded to see his normally impassive face frozen "into an expression of unbelieving horror" as he gazed at a point beside Gavin's right elbow. Gavin looked down to see the last coils of a snake as thick as his forearm brush past his shoulder and disappear into the reeds. Not many days after that Gavin was charged and nearly killed by a wild boar, but this seemed to me a mild experience in comparison.

Had I been on the constant look-out for snakes I would not have enjoyed our picnics on the banks – chicken sandwiches, hard-boiled eggs, oranges – or our evenings, when at dusk we moored on the edge of a lagoon and sat silent while storks, herons and eagles stained their feathers in the sunset or cruised against the dove-grey light. We had guns with us, and the Assistant MH seemed disappointed at my lack of enthusiasm for shooting our dinner, but I found the idea of slaughtering duck and pelican at odds with the nature of this particular expedition. He had no such inhibitions and I did not attempt to dissuade him.

I had little idea where we were most of the time and it was only after talking to Gavin and reading his notes that I was able to get even a rough notion. The area is virtually unmarked between the Euphrates villages of Huwair, Kabaish and Ramla, and the large lake southwest of Amara, fifty miles north. It is simply designated "marsh", with the Zikri lake in the middle of it. Some of it is rice country, its neat, watery terracing brilliant as glass, but mostly it consists of an endless fringe of reeds, now packed together, now straggling, with sudden sheets of lagoon. Although the feeling is of stillness, it is also one of immense suppressed vitality, the whole place humming with secret life. Birds take off without warning from where there was no sign of them, frogs begin bellowing for no apparent reason, ducks glide into the path of the boat, cicadas start up a chorus. From low down in the canoe the sky seems to close over one like an eyelid, veined with wisps of cloud and oyster-coloured. The reeds flutter and crack, every conceivable shade of green.

I cannot recall how we spent our nights, except that we were housed by sheikhs and that I drank a great deal of whisky, partly as a prophylactic, partly to ensure sleep. Nobody danced for us, as they did for Thesiger and Maxwell, but then we were not ministering to the population; simply looking.

I meant, after reading Gavin's book, to go back and do more than just flirt with the experience of the marshes. But in a way his marvellous evocation of them made it seem unnecessary. They were there in his pages for whenever I wanted to re-enter them, as I have just been doing.

Back in Baghdad I was put to work coordinating the labours of various subcommittees. Arthur was keen that his report should cover all eventualities and be complete before our return. Of Lofty there was now no sign.

We flew north one afternoon in a Viking to Mosul; the purpose of the excursion was to look over local schools but it also gave us a bird's-eye view of the pipeline that ran west from Kirkuk across the Syrian desert and ended on the Mediterranean at Haifa. From the air Iraq seemed dominated by its two silvery images, the twisting curves of the Tigris and the gentler arc of its oil lifeline. The sugary buildings of Baghdad – mosques, pylons, water towers, apartment blocks – floated beneath us in their noose of palms, already figments of mirage in the heat. As we flew on so did the desert take over, but always there remained the ochre glint of the Tigris, the flash of the pipeline and at intervals the puny flames from the fires that burned off the excess gases. Oil and water remained the constant equation.

Samara came and went, a blur of honey-coloured stone, and then the Tigris almost gave out, its shoals lying like the humps of hippopotamuses in a haggard river bed. Flying low, our wings shadowed families travelling on skins from the upper reaches, chattels stacked on their frail carriers. Sandstorms were common here, the sky blackening until visibility was reduced to an arm's length.

The pilot wanted to show us the extent of the Euphrates valley, where the rim of green cut off suddenly, so we turned west and then swung back over the holy city of Kadhimain, a flash of blue tile and gold dome in a nest of green. Gertrude Bell described Kadhimain as being bitterly pan-Islamic and anti-British, "a sheikh town with a very sacred mosque", which latter she found gimcrack and hideous. Above the city, dilapidation was less apparent; for all one could see, as though this were a cross-section in an architect's model, were arches and narrow, winding streets, palaces with pomegranates in their courtyards, the domes of mosques and the litter of bazaars. Encircling all this were the date palms, a rich lather of green suggestive of calm and refreshment.

Max Mallowan had been going up to Kirkuk to supervise a dig, and Gertrude Bell mentions a villa there and the recent finding of a hoard of tablets dating it as eighth century BC. "Kirkuk looked so agreeable with scarlet ranunculus on the edges of the green barley fields," she wrote one April in a letter to her father. But what we saw now as we approached was something altogether different, an absolutely modern oil town that seemed to have been deposited, preconstructed, in the desert. The pipeline led us first to it, skidding like a silver torpedo to the cluster of aluminium drums that made the place look like a giant observatory. Set apart from these, in neat rows, pink and yellow flat-roofed houses led off a palm-planted circus in all directions, like the spokes of a wheel. Each had its own garden, a swathe of orange, scarlet and mauve, which, beyond an enclosing wall, opened on to desert. There were no visible suburbs, simply the silver, red and blue metropolis of pipes, machinery and containers on the one side and the living quarters of their functionaries on the other.

We arrived at Mosul in a blaze of sunset, dipping over the Tigris, our wings laying bars of shadow on a honeycomb of mud houses. Our hotel was over the railway station and I thought how agreeable it would have been to have taken this journey by train, steaming slowly along the banks of the Tigris, with only a date oasis, an orange grove, a shepherd or two to distract one from the desert itself. Or alternatively to have gone south, crossing from Ctesiphon on the Tigris to Babylon on the Euphrates, the shimmer of the two rivers probing the desert like a pair of dividers. Ahead would be the gentle colonization of sand by water, lakes drying out and then reconstituting themselves as lagoons and marsh.

Mosul, apart from our hotel, seemed ancient and essentially Arab, a run-down city drugged by the scent of oranges and jasmin. After dinner I walked through the old town, dim lights burning in the huts, the smell of spices and woodsmoke drifting over the groups of huddled figures staring into the darkness. Some puffed at long-stemmed pipes, others crouched round charcoal fires in their goatskins and *abbas*, muffled to the eyes.

It was like coming on the tents of a marauding band, halted by nightfall outside a beleaguered city. The night was alive with hundreds of watching eyes, music wailing in the background, women sidling between the huts with whispers and flashing teeth. Oil might enrich a chosen few but it was not going to make much difference to the illiterate majority, moving from place to place, whipped up into nationalistic frenzy at opportune moments and then allowed to sink back into ignorance and poverty.

I strolled back to the hotel along the river, winding its way out under the moonlight towards Nineveh. Buffalo lay embedded in the glitter, dowagers in watery rhinestone, heavily motionless. A solitary dog began to bay, the yelping passed like a ball from animal to animal, until the quiet over the town was broken up into an irritation that went on all night.

After the morning's meeting we drove out to Nineveh. The walls of the ancient city were now grassed over or lying in ruin. Large slabs of concrete – one of them, cracked across its girth, bearing an enormous winged bull – afforded drying places for washing. Wheat like a green tide came flooding up to the foot of the walls, which were striped by the coloured wools of the women squatting in groups, spinning. On the skyline, just visible, though no more definite than clouds, the Kurdish hills rose lacy and white over the plains.

Like a lighthouse Jonah's mosque swept the surrounding country, the whalebone near the tomb a symbol of mortality. On the flat roofs of the houses carpets of dung dried out in the sun, wet garments billowed from lines as if still moulding flesh. In the dagger-bright sun dice clicked, cards were shuffled; so much time on the hands that could not be used any other way.

Outside Nineveh, among dried-out wadis and the humps of former encampments, now reduced to mummified existence, newer villages lay strewn about, all of them mud-built with reed roofs. Many of the children had pale skins, blue eyes and gingery-orange hair; strange offspring for the pipe-smoking old gentlemen swathed in goatskins who sat outside their huts over tiny cups of bitter coffee.

The children had no records of birth. Military doctors came round at intervals and assessed them, handing out an approximate age which in due course would render them elegible for service. Often the parents objected to the assessment and when they could afford it initiated lawsuits. But in the end there was no recourse. Sooner or later, understanding little, they would have to go. Since the early days of the Mandate progress had been steady in the setting up of schools, but already advances in liberal education were being threatened on all sides. The wars and revolutions that were the inevitable consequences of religious fanaticism were some years off, but the tide had begun to turn. In future, learning would be made subservient to prejudice and it would take brave men to fight for the intellectual independence of the institutions whose future we had spent the last few weeks planning.

A jackal accompanied my return to Mosul, galloping alongside the car. Gazelles sipped timidly at the edge of a roadside lake, lilac in the dusk, and in the distance a string of camels, myopic and supercilious, teetered long-sufferingly into the desert, members of the great nomadic herds who carried their civilization wearily, like loads, on their backs. On every wall on the outskirts of Mosul nationalistic slogans had been daubed, half-illegible for the half-illiterate. It did not take much prescience to realize who would be the sufferers when the money ran out and the slogans came home to roost.

That night the wind got up for the first time since we had

arrived, rattling sand against the windows. Outside, the domes of the mosques looked frozen by moonlight. I had seen snow on the blue Kurdish hills and the storks overhead seemed thefts of ice.

We returned to Baghdad for final meetings with our hosts. I concocted a résumé of our activities, and draft proposals for action on the architectural and administrative fronts were circulated.

Arthur and Sir Charles returned to London together. I had dinner one night with the Mallowans, during most of which Agatha seemed preoccupied or broody. Next morning Hugh called for me and in high spirits we took off for what we knew in the Navy as a "Friday Wild".

"What do you want to see?" Hugh asked as we gained height over Baghdad and I said the latest and the oldest. So we flew east into the Badiet Esh Sham along the pipeline, a flashing thermometer stretching from horizon to horizon, and then swung back to follow the Euphrates on its way into the marshes above Basra. From the air all sense of complexity and secretiveness was lost; the water spilled from its green coverlet into hundreds of friendly canals. We skimmed low over Bumugeraifat, to whose name Arthur had taken a fancy, and made the boars run near Al Madina. The buffaloes, pale liquorice-coloured in the noon light, never twitched an eyelid, the river clothing them like nightgowns and leaving only their snouts visible.

Soon we were over the Shatt al Arab, Abadan and Khoramshahr to port as we shadowed the islands of the Gulf. Thirty-five years later this would be frontier country in an endless war, but now it seemed to ooze contentment and money. Mosques, palaces, ruins, oases, herds of cattle, forts passed under our plane like the furnishings of a great game, its moves begun an eternity ago and its outcome still in doubt.

The weekend was everything that Hugh had promised: expeditions, feasting, music, dancing, and refined versions of those pleasures that poor old Lofty had so humiliatingly failed to provide.

Back in London it was the marsh light that I would remember, that explosive silence and whisper, the slap of water against the sides of the boat. I had no illusions that my British Council career would contain many distractions of this sort and in the remaining three years of it I never once set foot outside our Grosvenor Square offices on duty. Arthur Morgan had his wings clipped and there was a general feeling of retrenchment within the Council itself.

My own department had its share of characters. There was Laurence Lacey, for example, a dapper figure who habitually wore spotted bow ties. He used to amuse himself by simulating epileptic fits in front of innocent secretaries, frightening the life out of them. Having pretended to froth over his handkerchief and writhed about on the floor, he would suddenly leap to his feet and depart as if nothing had happened. What began as an obscure charade went too far and he was sacked.

Denis Long, who had fought in North Africa and Greece and retired as a captain, soon made it plain that he was in no mood for further regimentation. Cynically disposed towards most of the Council's activities, but with recognizable moral values of his own, he poked paternalistic fun at the female staff, carrying out his duties with an attentiveness that fell just short of insolence. On Saturdays we played cricket together for the Council, humping our bags to obscure suburban grounds. It was a miracle if all those selected turned up within an hour of the appointed time, which was irritating for our opponents, though they usually got the better of us. A saturnine, endearing figure, Denis departed from the Council soon after I did. Temperamentally attuned to disaster and disappointment he subsequently enjoyed his fair share of both, before ending up in one of Tyneside's social service departments and earning himself the OBE.

Most of us worked in the same airy room overlooking Grosvenor Square. My secretary and assistant on the magazine, not in her first youth, fell in love with a bald hairdresser, an expert on Latin American dancing. Together they spun their evenings away together in *palais de danse*, quick-quick-slow, her rather respectable and modest appearance at odds with her chosen sport and her lover's subsequent wig.

Since our department's activities were largely concerned with the welfare of foreign students we had a van of our own, its function being to convey students to lodgings and appointments and to meet them on arrival at stations or airports. This van was occasionally borrowed by other members of staff, for their own pleasure. Hyde Park at that time was awash from dusk onwards with prostitutes; you could see them at work from the van, flashes of stocking, bare thigh and suspender, like exotic mushrooms against almost every tree, while an admiring circle of onlookers studied the action from a range of a few yards. No sooner had one customer departed than another hopped in, the circle never thinning though the clientele changed. From a distance it must have seemed as inexplicable a ritual as something out of Kafka.

The erotic excitement generated by these parading women, affording a *passeggiata* of a peculiarly English kind, became too much for a member of another department. He became friendly with the regular driver of the van, borrowing it late at night to entice selected women off their beats, often in twos and threes. He would drive with friends to an appealing spot, preferably with a pleasant view of the Serpentine, and there lay out food and drink, after which the girls would perform. News of these *déjeuners sur l'herbe* soon spread, and the travelling circus acquired a variety of distinguished customers.

Another member of the department was Dashwood Evans, the courier. An ex-sailor, bodyguard and one-time companion to several celebrated homosexuals, he was part scoundrel, part charmer. Used to living on his wits he was game for anything, genuinely concerned for the well-being of his charges but, under an innocently boyish manner, highly versed in the ways of the world.

It might seem, from the congregation of such disparate characters, each trying to find his feet, as I was, in a civilian world where the future was not underwritten, that a community spirit would suffer. In fact, the atmosphere in our room was not unlike that below decks in a ship, each person having his own tasks outside the mess, and the mess itself affording light relief and the chance for an exchange of views. Elsewhere in the department there was a preponderance of women, acolytes of its head who had pronounced leanings towards her own sex.

My own life was now beginning to take a different turn. Alan Pryce-Jones, for whom I was writing regularly in *The Times Literary Supplement*, took me one night to an after-dinner party at Cyril Connolly's house. Sitting on the floor was a girl with huge dark eyes and long dark hair, wearing a black dress. Some months later we would be married. On that same evening Cyril, one of whose most engaging qualities was the trouble he would take when his interest was aroused, spent a long time away from the party showing me round his library. He took books out from the shelves very gently, as if fearful of bruising them. I had written a longish article on Nathanael West earlier in the year which *Horizon* had published and now Cyril gave me all Scott Fitzgerald's novels on which to do a similar piece. That night was not only memorable for my meeting Jennifer Fry and for the start of a rewarding, occasionally interrupted relationship with Cyril that lasted until his death nearly thirty years later; it was also the occasion on which I first met Anthony and Violet Powell, Patrick Kinross and Henry Green, all of whom became close friends.

Charles Wrey Gardiner was still running the Grey Walls Press, though his partner Peter Baker, a Conservative MP, had gone inside for fraud. I persuaded Charles to take on Nathanael West and Scott Fitzgerald and their complete works came out in agreeable editions, though on indifferent paper. Later Secker & Warburg, and in the United States Farrar, Straus & Giroux, produced one-volume editions of West with my *Horizon* essay as introduction. Paul Scott was the firm's accountant, a quiet unobtrusive figure with no apparent literary ambitions.

Ring Lardner was the next American novelist to engage my attention and I was able to encourage Chatto & Windus to publish a volume of his best stories with a preface by myself. This, too, found an American publisher, Scribner's taking it on. It was odd that such dealings, concerning American writers, should come about this way round.

It became gradually clear to me that if I was to have the kind of writing life I wanted, though had scarcely expected to afford, I should have to leave the Council. There was no future for me overseas, since I had no teaching experience, and no qualifications for that matter, and a nine-to-six job in Grosvenor Square running a students' newsletter would not take me far, nor allow me much time for writing.

Kurdish Shepherds

They squat silhouetted against the hills,
A handful of men with rifles, sharp-nosed
And dark, in pale blue turbans whose frills
Hang down on them, as if they were posed.

They might have been there forever, lost
In their spiritual mnemonics, herds grazing
At will or wandering beneath them on mossed
And irregular plains – till sunset drops in a flare,
Illumining them, making their world amazing.

Basra: Experiments with Oil

Oilwells and palms; silver tassels of pylons; dhows
Adrift on olive and gilded water, like carcasses of birds,
Their wings blown into sails; banks of buffalo
Testing the sluggish current; boats embedded in reeds,
With patches of startling green round the trunks
Of the date trees – round all these the afternoon sinks
And curdles, an ochre-stained landscape of junk.

Villages of mud, like plasticine models, are clamped
Over leaking shores, where, for miles, the flatness exudes
Avenues of sumptuous dirt, and the skyline is stamped
With the frescoing smoke of the docks. Heavily, broods
Of pelican and crane take off from the marshes,
Aeroplanes stream in over wheatfields in flood.
Now they've found oil, cracked smiles in the desert break
Through the gravel: steel drills, like flowers, grow
Branches on mud; only custom is anywhere at stake.

Student Riots in the Middle East

The real inciters are never seen – they exist
By imaginary need or whispered orders.
And fed through channels of petty adventure,
These half-grown men riot, till one of them is killed.
Then causes evaporate; just the dead persist.

Flying over Baghdad

Water towers; the river; the golden tombs
Of Kadhimain; and wider, beyond the city,
Circles of green with fountaining branches
Of leaves and dates. Sand craters, like bombs

96

That have missed their mark, lie out in trenches,
   Where the tilted wingspan
Of sight crowds the whole town to an entity.

But the view is deceptive. We struggle
For poise in the air, and leave in our slipstream
Hills starched under snow, the straggle
Of huts round the river; and sun like a cream
Melting over palaces. Pipelines tell us more,
   Lining the Tigris with money,
Heaping promises like sand, and, as easily, war.

Not that poverty means happiness,
The picturesque past something to look back
On with credit. But now, as glittering and less,
Baghdad flashes its *arriviste* suburbs
Under us, elbowing out villages, the lack
   Of a synthesis grows brutally
Evident. Ignorance and greed futilely trying to tally.

And what we see here, a fragmentary
Culture unwrapped on an auburn morning,
Its legacies of luxury, squalor, and unnecessary
Suffering, ought to remind us – a warning
Against digging our toes in, overloading fate
   With avarice; till, forced to it,
Mobs move on us, like great rivers in spate.

Taking Off from Kirkuk Aerodrome

The Dove with its silver eyelids climbs and turns
Through parabolas of blue
The whole sky
Askew

And behind us the pipeline stretches and burns.
At intervals oil is ignited, fire
Burning off gases
Below
As, air-bound, we alter course northwards and feel
Persia like a crust rising
To meet us,
Snow
Now the route we fly over and probe like a weal.

Museum of Antiquities, Baghdad

The stages can all be seen, rubbed clear of their dirt –
At first only crude but wonderful mosaics, the clumsy
Efforts at communication, where writing is simply
A bird or a tree, with words whose curt
   Meaning comes from an alphabet
Entirely pictorial: the pure draughtsman's intellect.

Then, later, embellishment; chalices and figurines, women
And men portrayed as their genitals. Snaked rings
Symbolizing ritual, and bellams whose curved prows
Paraphrase travel. Carved scenes emphasizing
   Luxury, feluccas and dhows
Flushed in the sunset of more finished specimens.

But, mostly, the glazed pots and bitumen bowls
Convey only essentials; details were regarded as rhetoric,
Decorations superfluous to their necessary roles
Of enlarging awareness. The real achievement
   Of these fragmentary, written-on relics
Is immediacy, their beautiful economy of statement.

PART III

Drinkers and Dandies

I LEFT THE COUNCIL IN 1951, after four years, to embark on the life of a freelance journalist. I had no confidence that I would ever make a living out of the writing of books, since I wanted to write poetry most of all, but I had done regular reviewing at various times for the *New Statesman*, *The Times Literary Supplement* and the *Observer*, and I was a frequent contributor to the Third Programme. I knew only too well how easily such sources of income can dry up. A change of editor, or simply an editor's need for change, is all that is necessary. But I had a bit of luck at this point which completely altered my life.

One evening we were invited to dinner by Jim and Pam Rose to meet Harold Nicolson. Jim was at that time literary editor of the *Observer* and Harold had reviewed *Time Was Away*, the Corsican book from my trip with Johnny Minton, very generously, so I was looking forward to the evening. *Some People* had long been one of my favourite books.

There were two consequences to that dinner. The more predictable was a friendship with Harold that lasted until his death. The other, resulting from a chance remark to Jim Rose, was an association with the *Observer* that lasted for over twenty years.

I had complained to Jim that the *Observer*, like most papers of similar quality, maintained two standards of writing: one for the political, foreign and arts pages, and another for the sports pages. This was particularly true of soccer, for while one writer of quality was generally recognized as being essential to cover cricket, and possibly also rugby and golf, no such interest was shown in football writing. At this time there were sports writers around of the stature of Neville Cardus and Robertson-Glasgow, Jim Swanton and Leonard Crawley, and, on rugby, Vivian Jenkins. Soccer was the poor relation, except when it came to the work of the lushly romantic Geoffrey Green on *The Times*, and the wily Dai Davies, soon to be retired from his post as "Old International" on the *Manchester Guardian*.

The Sunday papers relied largely on agency reports. The *Observer*, for example, had a dear old fellow called Jimmy Bolton, who came from Bolton as it happened. He must have been doing the job for donkey's years, but he did not only do it for the *Observer*. On any match day he would expect to be reporting for anything up to half a dozen provincial daily or evening papers. The mechanics of this required the use of many carbons, each one containing a slightly different intro but essentially the same as the others, and much telephoning. As a result, Jimmy scarcely had time to watch the game at all. When he was not putting a fresh carbon into his ancient machine or tapping away, he was dictating run-of-play stuff to a telephonist in Wolverhampton or Newcastle. It was physically impossible, shrewd and experienced observer of the game as he was, for him to do more than record the names of goal scorers – often missing the incident itself – and the size of the crowd.

It seemed to me that the *Observer* ought to aim a bit higher than this; that the pattern of play, its tactics, style, skill, individual characters deserved the same kind of attention as in cricket. Apart from Jimmy's own piece in the *Observer*, under the by-line J. T. Bolton, all other match reports were "By our own correspondent" – i.e. agency.

Having said all this to Jim Rose I thought no more about

it. At that time I used to watch Charlton Athletic, then in the First Division, every other Saturday with Roy and Kate Fuller and Julian and Kathleen Symons, whose families shared a house in St John's Park, Blackheath. On the Saturday Charlton were away I would travel up on the Underground from South Kensington to White Hart Lane. While much else fades from my memory, the Spurs and Charlton players of the late '40s and early '50s, with their individual manner of playing and their physical idiosyncrasies, survive intact. Although I had been at a rugby-playing school, my passion for soccer, acquired on my arrival in England from India at the age of seven, had not faded. In the spring term at Haileybury we ran an eleven of sorts, reproducing the more elaborate and stylish effects of the professional game, observed in the holidays, as well as we were able. I can still remember one brilliant March afternoon when I swerved my way through the mud and drove a left-foot shot from 25 yards into the top of the net. The glow lasted until the first net of the new cricket season.

About a fortnight after that evening at the Roses' I had a call from Harold Gale, Sports Editor of the *Observer*. Would I like to call in one day with a view to doing the occasional football report?

In my mind's eye I see Harold in a wing collar and spats. I don't suppose he actually wore either, but he looked as if he ought to have done. He certainly seemed to belong to a much earlier generation and style of sports writing. Once upon a time he had been a snooker champion, and he looked right for the world of billiard saloons, of green baize, bright lights and sleeves regulated by elastic over the biceps.

I was given one or two amateur matches to cover, at a time when amateur soccer, with the rise of Pegasus, the talented Oxford and Cambridge side, was having one of its last great moments. Then it was Wembley time, for the amateur cup and the FA Cup. I presumed Jimmy Bolton would be covering both matches. But just before the first of them was due to take place he had some kind of accident, whether real or tactful I never could discover. In his place I reported the victory of Wellington over Bishop Auckland and a week later that of Arsenal, playing in old gold, over Liverpool. The Arsenal team that day was Swindon, Scott, Barnes, Forbes, Compton, L., Mercer, Cox, Logie, Goring, Lewis and Compton, D. Lewis scored both their goals and the match was dominated by the wing-half play of Forbes and Mercer.

That was the start of my four years as the *Observer*'s association football correspondent, ended only by my succeeding Robertson-Glasgow as cricket correspondent, a job that took me abroad most winters.

I was initially paid absurdly little but I would have done it for expenses. The build-up to Saturday, with the early-morning journey to Old Trafford, Villa Park, Molyneux or wherever it might be, the intellectual exercise of trying to finish a 700-word analysis of the play while at the same time re-creating the atmosphere and the tension, within ten minutes of the final whistle, was exciting and stimulating. I had the chance to see something of Midland and Northern towns I might otherwise have missed and I had a privileged seat from which to watch the great players of the day, such as Stanley Matthews, Tom Finney, Stanley Mortensen, Alf Ramsey, Wilf Mannion and Billy Wright.

The Spurs had dropped down to the Second Division in the late '40s but my arrival as a football writer coincided with the start of their glory years. They won promotion to the First Division and the First Division championship in successive years and they played thrilling football. It was fortunate for me that they did so, because I was able to justify my frequent visits to White Hart Lane on the grounds that they were the most exciting team in the country. Harold Gale indulged me perhaps rather more than he should have done, but then he was a kindly man with a relaxed attitude to his duties. Jimmy Bolton, when I saw him again, bore me no grudge for having usurped his position at the *Observer*. All it really meant was that now he had only to do four simultaneous reports instead of five.

No sooner had I covered my first Cup Final than I began my stint as No. 2 to Robertson-Glasgow on the cricket pages. Three years later, on an August afternoon, that brilliant, generous and graceful writer, cursed with manic depression, took his leave of the game and not many years later his own life. From 1953 to 1972 I did my best not to seem too much of a let-down.

Sports journalism was now providing me with a modest income and also with a subject. My experiences in Iraq had got me writing poetry again and I wanted now to try to write poems in which football and cricket were seen in their social context. I had visions of a poetry that would be classless, and at the same time accessible to people who had never cared for poetry or even considered it as something worth their attention.

My work for the *Observer* occupied only Saturdays, and although I was still doing occasional reviews for various papers I had time on my hands. I found I missed the obligation of regular work.

Cyril Connolly had recently undertaken to translate a 400 page book by Philippe Diolé on underwater archaeology. Predictably, after doing one chapter, he got bored with it and suggested to the publishers that I take it over. I was happy to do so and for the next three years provided myself with an office life of my own, translating not only *The Underwater Adventure* and another book by Diolé, *The Seas of Sicily*, but also a book about fetishism in West Africa, *The Sacred Forest*. Denis Long, temporarily out of a job, helped me with the last of these, typing while I dictated. Some of the fetishistic activities were so gruesomely comical that it was impossible to take them seriously.

George Weidenfeld had, the year before, started the magazine *Contact*, for which I wrote a series of pieces on aspects of London – a day trip to Southend; Charing Cross Road noticeboards, on which "special services" were advertised – and soon he was to start his publishing firm. At about this time I had become interested in the novels of Charles-Louis Philippe, who had died in 1909 aged 35.

Philippe was of peasant origin, a native of Cerilly, a village in the Bourbonnais, and his novels were set either there or in the poor quarters of Paris. There was in existence a translation by Violet Hudson of *Marie Donadieu*, but his most celebrated novel, *Bubu de Montparnasse*, about a Parisian prostitute, had never appeared in England. Laurence Vail had done a version for Caresse Crosby's Continental Editions, which was published in Paris in 1932, but for some reason – censorship, perhaps – it had never made the crossing.

George was keen to issue the book in a series of illustrated classics and I undertook to revise and de-Americanize Vail's version. Leonard Rosoman, whose work as a war artist I had always greatly admired and whom I had come to know through William Sansom, did some elegant drawings; perhaps too elegant for Philippe's bitter realism.

Philippe was held in high regard by T. S. Eliot, who tellingly described him as both compassionate and dispassionate. Germans of the Grosz and Brecht generations thought him a neglected master. Neither Communists nor Catholics could justly claim him after his death as one of theirs, though both tried. He was simply one of the poor, who wrote about the poor as an equal, tenderly but without sentimentality. He saw society in much the same terms as did Grosz and Brecht – the workers reduced to squalor while capitalists flourished obscenely – but he had no doctrinaire solutions.

Philippe's work was essentially autobiographical and documentary in nature – "*Philippe était loin d'être un aigle*," Apollinaire observed in a letter – and *Bubu* is simply his own story, that of a country bumpkin who falls in love with a gentle girl of the streets. Through her he becomes familiar with the world of pimps and criminals, of degradation and disease.

"I find it extraordinary," Philippe observed, "that the novel is being used for social and psychological studies. I do not believe a writer has to have education. For myself, if you want to know my most urgent feeling, it is this: I have a sense of class." It was the dignity of that class-consciousness, one that had nothing to do with politics, that gave all Philippe's writing a rugged beauty.

Bubu was widely and favourably reviewed and I was pleased to have been associated with it.

Earlier that year, in pursuit of a vaguely formulated scheme of writing a book about Mediterranean islands which had been associated in one way or another with Nelson, I had spent some weeks in the Gulf of Naples. Partly a journal, partly an account of what various travellers had to say about the area – Boccaccio, Chateaubriand, Stendhal, Lamartine, Edward Lear – the book came out, also from Weidenfeld & Nicolson, under the slightly misleading title of *The Gulf of Pleasure*.

Gavin Ewart had been in Naples during the war, and now no longer an employee of either *Poetry London* or the British Council – he departed at about the same time as Denis Long and myself – he contributed a poem to the anthological part of the book and helped me with translations from Latin and Italian. In due course Gavin went into advertising, and it was surprising, in view of his later subject matter, that he preferred to write technical copy about tractors to more lyrical pieces about products for women. His reluctance to be involved in television limited his future, but what television lost poetry in due course gained.

At that time Gavin was mainly known for his poem about

Miss Twye soaping her breasts in the bath and for a couple of war poems, "Officer's Mess" and "When a Beau Goes In". He had written very few poems during the war and the decade that followed and he needed a lot of stoking up to get going again. Once he had started there was no holding him. When, in 1965, I started my own firm it was a special pleasure to publish Gavin's two volumes *Pleasures of the Flesh* and *The Deceptive Grin of the Gravel Porters*, for we had been friends since *Poetry London* days and shared many interests, cricket, squash and stories about Tambimuttu among them.

There is in most writers a detectable relationship between their physical appearance and their way of writing. In Gavin's case there was none at all; the fluency, wit and stylistic virtuosity, as well as the obsessively sexual preoccupations of his poems, were in stark contrast to his stolidity of figure, slowness of speech and general deliberateness. Lunching with him was always enjoyable except that one usually got through three courses while he was still on his soup.

Gavin devoted many months during his years of poetic abstinence to a futuristic novel containing pornographic goings-on in Buckingham Palace, but there was never any likelihood of its seeing the light of day. It was typical of Gavin that he could not be convinced of this and was prepared to waste time over more and more elaborate fantasies. Similarly, he remains curiously undiscriminating about his own poetry. When a third volume was due I wanted to leave out what seemed to me the least successful poems but Gavin would have none of it. His view was that everything should go in and the reader should be left free to reject what he didn't care for. I tried to persuade Gavin that this would weaken the impact of the better poems but he remained unconvinced and took the book elsewhere. We had no quarrel about it and I never come across Gavin without an involuntary smile of affection.

Few weeks went by during the early '50s when I did not see Henry Green and William Sansom. Both had been in the Fire Service during the war and both had written much-praised books about their experiences, Green a novel called *Caught* and Sansom a volume of short stories called *Fireman Flower*. They were in different ways equally eccentric, their mannered prose reflective of unusual perceptions and idiosyncratic attitudes.

I had often met Henry at John Lehmann's house in Egerton Crescent and he had been a recent admirer of my wife. He was at that time immensely handsome, in the dark, romantic fashion suggested by Matthew Smith's portrait of him, and extremely funny. He appeared to be totally unliterary and most comfortable with anecdotes to do with his years on the shop floor of his father's engineering factory, as described in *Living*. With women to whom he was attracted he adopted a teasing manner, never appearing to take them seriously but putting himself out to entertain. At the same time he drew them out, demanding revelations, indiscreet gossip, accounts of disaster.

Henry's ancient father was still alive at the time and Henry himself spent his days at the firm's offices off Baker Street, every so often paying visits to the works in Birmingham. He imported Goronwy Rees into the firm. His father's continued presence was evidently a burden and Henry used to imitate him shuffling across his room, transferring a paper from one desk to another and then a few minutes later taking it back again. When his father finally retired, or perhaps died in office, Henry breathed more freely. But the firm unfortunately did not prosper under Henry and it was not long before he himself withdrew, falling into a rapid physical decline which was accelerated by gin.

The deterioration was sad to behold, only a few years encompassing the change from an amusing, striking-looking man of the world, equally successful, it appeared, as novelist and industrialist, to a tottering, unshaven recluse, hard of hearing, short of breath and teeth, who nevertheless lingered on for another twenty years.

In the '50s Henry was probably the most critically admired novelist in the country. The Americans, too, had suddenly tuned into his particular brand of devious high comedy, his ability to make dialogue tell the story, his skill in switching from working-class vernacular and pub conversation to sophisticated romantic banter. So much so that Henry and his wife Dig set off by liner, accompanied by a lawyer, for New York, there to be fêted and written up, and Henry's picture – at least the back of his head – appeared in *Time* magazine. It was one of his foibles that he refused to be photographed in public except from the back, so that the most familiar public image of him was of gleaming black hair, as in the painting by Magritte.

Henry, a generous host, had otherwise an odd attitude towards money, a fear of being exploited, perhaps, which accounted for the presence of his lawyer. Not really surprisingly, no great sums of money resulted from the American editions of Henry's books, and though he had many distinguished admirers there among novelists and critics, he was essentially too poetic and experimental, too English a writer in his social perceptiveness, to attract an American public in large numbers.

The consequent let-down affected Henry, whose expectations had been unrealistically aroused. His novels had been getting steadily more abstract, so that they read almost like plays, and, as suggested by their titles, *Doting, Concluding, Nothing*, thinner in content. Now they stopped altogether. He had done most of his writing in the early evening, after returning from the office, and the end of office life seemed to result in the end of life for him altogether. For a few months Henry toyed with a kind of autobiographical book, a sequel to *Pack My Bag*, in which his passion for billiards as a young man was a developing theme, but it did not get very far.

I never remember Henry in anything other than a dark grey suit and sober tie. He wore a trilby in the street and carried or wore a dark raincoat. He was as deeply conventional in his appearance and views, as fearful of drawing attention in person, as he was adventurous in his writing. There is no more beautiful prose in the language, evocative, mysteriously suggestive, gravely tender, than some of the passages in *Caught*, *Loving* and *Back*.

Henry was an amused man, rarely serious in his conversation. Yet he could talk brilliantly about writing when he was in the mood, generally late at night and after some drink. I remember an evening in Trevor Place, where he lived, when he outlined his theories about reducing the novel to abstraction, in a similar way to that in which painters were working, elaborating them over several hours in a fashion of which you would never have expected him capable, largely because he was so unpretentious in manner, apparently so unconcerned with theory and philosophical speculation. His favourite topic of conversation in later years was the behaviour of cats, a source of never-ending fascination and entertainment to himself if not often to his friends.

Curiously, since he was an addictive reader of conventional novels, the writers whose style he most admired were Céline and the Doughty of *Arabia Deserta*. A secretive, mysterious man, he liked best to drink with a variety of saloon-bar cronies of no obvious interest to outsiders. Arthur Koestler was a late friend and John Sutro an early one, but Henry, unmistakably patrician himself in voice and bearing, found people of different background and interests to his own the source of most pleasure. It was his ear for the submerged music of their unexpressed thoughts, his sympathy for their relationships and clumsy conversation, that gave his novels their peculiar splendour.

Once when Henry was on a business visit to Birmingham and there was a Test Match at Edgbaston I invited him into the press box. He was greatly amused to find himself next to Jack Hobbs's "ghost", the great man himself being on his ghost's other side. While play was going on the ghost would feed Jack various questions, about tactics, the technique of a particular batsman or bowler, and Jack would make wry, slightly dismissive comments on their shortcomings. The ghost would dutifully tap these out on his typewriter, handing the copy to Jack for approval before passing it to the messenger for telephoning through to the office. Jack would read through what he had himself said during the day but, faced with seeing his criticisms in print, would often withdraw them all. "Oh, let's just say he's a very promising young player but with a bit to learn." The ghost would then patiently scrunch up the day's work and improvise some bland comments on his own. Jack's name on the article was enough; it never really mattered what he said.

Another time Henry came to watch a Test at Headingley and afterwards I drove him out into the country for drinks and supper. As we passed an extremely out-of-the way and isolated inn called The Tiger, hidden between two hills, Henry remarked amusedly, "Sebastian always brings me here, it's one place he can be certain no one will ever see us and embarrass him". Sebastian, Henry's son, had at that time recently joined the family firm and was based in Leeds. Very like Henry to look at and in manner, he proved a better business man than his father, with a talent for bridge and a taste for glamorous sports cars.

Henry was no traveller, and apart from his brief American adventure I can only once remember him going abroad. One August we rented the Villa Hanbury at La Mortola, just across the Italian frontier. We invited Bill Sansom and Henry and Dig, as well as Violet and Francis Wyndham. Amazingly, Dig managed to prevail on Henry to accept. On the first day he came down to the beach with everyone else, but one visit was enough for him. For the rest of his stay he spent the mornings sitting by a lily pond under the terrace with a glass of gin in his hand. At intervals he would get up and prod with a stick at a water snake that lurked under the leaves. Eventually the exasperated snake reared out of the water, coiling itself round the stick and giving Henry a nasty fright.

The gardens at La Mortola, spilling down to the sea, contained a great many rare plants. At their highest point, where the southern route from France into Italy bordered the Hanbury property, there was a famous and extremely expensive hotel-restaurant. While we were there it was taken over for a few days by King Farouk, one-time lover of Cyril Connolly's wife Barbara Skelton, and his entourage, many of whom were armed. For several days beforehand Farouk's unpleasant-looking guards roamed around the gardens as if they were their own property. Attempts to shift them met with no response and the local *carabinieri* declined to take any action.

Henry used to wander around the gardens glass in hand, and when one lunch time there was no sign of him I was alarmed that he might have fallen down one of the many ravines. We came upon him eventually, sitting in a clearing with a group of guards, their rifles laid aside. Henry and the guards were silently grinning at each other, an empty gin bottle in front of them.

Bill Sansom was even more of a worry, because when he was drinking he became idiotically provocative. It was his habit on seeing one of the guards to greet or toast him in a variety of languages, all of them incomprehensible to the Egyptians. These greetings were often accompanied by exaggeratedly formal gestures. It was plain that the guards were uncertain how to react. They seemed to comprehend that they were faced by an eccentric of some kind, but had no means of knowing whether he was mocking them or trying to be friendly. One night we were awoken by wild firing. Bill, unable to sleep, had gone out for some fresh air but had tripped over a wheelbarrow. The guards, dozing in a group under their master's window, were awoken by the clatter and, fearing an assassin had made his way in from the sea, blazed randomly into the darkness. Bill kept to the terrace after that.

Henry and Bill were long-time friends, but I doubt whether they ever had a meal together on their own initiative. They lived on opposite sides of London and were the kind of people, solitary in their work, who needed prodding from others to budge. Henry was by seven years the older of the two and in literary terms belonged to another generation. At the end of the war Henry was forty, Bill thirty-three. By the time Bill acquired some sort of public recognition, with his first novel, *The Body*, published in 1949, Henry had already written his best books and begun to run out of material. Between 1945 and the appearance of the first novels of Kingsley Amis and Alan Sillitoe, and of the plays of John Osborne, Bill was among the most prolific and admired of writers whose careers began during the war.

It was only after he had joined the fire service as a full-time fireman on the outbreak of war that Bill had started writing. He had worked briefly as a bank clerk, as an advertising copywriter and as a pianist in a club, so he said. He always seemed to me a terrible pianist, making whatever he played sound exactly the same, but perhaps the customers weren't fussy. Bill's father had been a naval architect, designing ships for the Russians as well as the Germans, and as a boy, before and after a spell at Uppingham, Bill had travelled all over Europe with him. I have on my desk as I write a silver anchor, given to me by Bill, a souvenir of one of his father's enterprises.

I must have first met Bill at John Lehmann's. He was then living in Swiss Cottage, at Buckland Crescent, and I, having left the Vaughan–Minton household, was nearby in Cavendish Avenue. My flatmate Vera was a friend of the fashion artist Ruth Sheradski, with whom Bill spent weekends. Bill's ground-floor flat opened on to a large garden, the lawn of which he rarely cut. As a result it was like looking on to a

Douanier Rousseau jungle, through which at dusk bare-breasted women sometimes stalked. The flat itself was infested with snails, whose slimy trails left Jackson Pollock-like markings all over his floorboards.

Whatever deprivations in the way of cooking, comfort and company Bill may have suffered during the week were amply compensated for when he was with Ruth at her home in Chelsea. She gave elaborate dinner parties, encouraged his latent dandyism and was never other than sweetly solicitous and gentle. The fashion world in which Ruth moved – inhabited by designers such as Bunny Roger and Digby Morton, and by photographers like John French and Peter Rose Pulham – was never much to Bill's taste and he ended up becoming increasingly drunk and truculent. Sadly for all their friends their long relationship ended abruptly; Bill left Ruth Sheradski on a Saturday morning to go shopping and never returned. He rang us up that night at 1 a.m. to announce rather drunkenly that he was getting married. "I'll put you over to Ruth", he said, handing the telephone, so I thought, to Ruth Sheradski. But it was another Ruth who spoke, also rather drunkenly: an actress called Ruth Grundy. Bill did indeed marry her, and for a while they seemed very happy. They moved to Hamilton Terrace, had a son and generally prospered. But Ruth, though initially attractive and lively, unfortunately became as heavy a drinker as Bill, who would veer between complete abstinence and alcoholic bouts lasting several days. Soon the fur began to fly, and long before Bill died they were tearing each other to pieces. The last time I saw him, when he was in hospital with various complaints including terrible ulcers on his legs, he showed me a note left for him with the ward sister. It was from Ruth. "I have torn up and thrown away all your notebooks, diaries and manuscripts, so if you ever come out you won't find anything."

Of the more interesting writers of his generation Bill has suffered the most severe eclipse. I am not sure why this should be so, except that he was rather mannered in much, though not all, of his work. His early volumes of stories, *Fireman Flower* and *Something Terrible, Something Lovely*, were certainly influenced by Kafka, a sense of undefined threat hanging over many of the characters. But with each book the Kafka resemblance diminished, Bill's own loving eye for topographical detail, his pleasure in the macabre and the bizarre, his delight in unusual words and people, combining to produce a flow of stories quite unlike anyone else's. His prose was cumulative in effect, the result of minute observations recorded in not quite the way one would expect.

In 1949 Bill published his first novel, *The Body*, which had a jacket by Ruth Sheradski. This part-hilarious, part-tragic study of a hairdresser driven crazy by jealousy became the *Evening Standard* Book of the Month, taking Bill into quite a different readership. He began to write more simply, often very comically; menace and disquiet were now replaced by quirkiness of behaviour, oddness of predicament. In a Sansom story setting counts for as much as character and it is scrutinized and described with a miniaturist's passion. The characters tend to be conventional, rather dull people, whose humdrum lives are totally changed by a sudden slight shift of circumstance. I don't recall Bill ever writing about men or women of much worldly consequence; certainly not about intellectuals, artists or high-powered professional people. What his characters are, in fact, rarely matters, what count are the intense feelings which they harbour and which drive them to uncharacteristic and strange acts. All writers are to an extent voyeurs, but Bill, in his concentrated, pressurized way, was more so than most; he was sleuth-like in his efforts to pick up clues, relentless in his pursuit of evidence.

Bill always carried a notebook and he was not shy of producing it to jot down something he had just thought of, heard or seen. When he was writing he would jig one foot up and down, like a Bengali tailor or bazaar vendor. I used to do the same.

116

After the success of *The Body*, Bill began to get lucrative commissions for travel articles. His fare paid, he managed to use these journeys also to write fictionalized travel sketches. These were collected in two volumes, *South* and *The Passionate North*, both remarkable for their skill in suggesting light, climate and landscape, and at the same time telling a convincing story with convincing foreign characters.

By the early 1960s Bill had written three more novels, more travel pieces, a book of ballads, and a large number of stories. These last were collected in a volume called *The Stories of William Sansom* and published in 1963 with a long introduction by Elizabeth Bowen. "The writer has taken," she wrote, "and shown himself right in taking, a succession of calculated risks. He is not writing *for* effect, he is dealing *in* it, and masterfully."

By now only V. S. Pritchett was comparable in talent as a writer of stories. There were two more collections, *The Ulcerated Milkman* and *The Marmalade Bird*, published seven years apart, but apart from the wonderful story "Down at the Hydro", the stories of his last years lacked the strangeness and tension, the hallucinatory quality of his best work. The tone became obtrusively whimsical, playful in the faintly tiresome manner that Bill put on when he was getting drunk.

His behaviour in a bad mood was boring and indefensible. At one stage he was always being sick. During the brief reign of Malcolm Muggeridge at *Punch* I undertook to do a piece on the Miss World contest and foolishly took Bill along to the ceremony. At the crucial moment, after the rattle of drums and in the silence before the announcement of the winners, I was appalled to hear the unmistakable preliminaries to Bill's throwing up. For about ten seconds there was no other sound in the place. Then, the vomit neatly deposited in his brown bowler, he was as right as rain and ready for the action. The ushers were less well disposed, and politely but firmly we were requested to leave. Only Philip Toynbee threw up more often and in more places than Bill.

It was not always as bad as that. I had to go into the London Clinic about the same time for a minor operation and Bill insisted on accompanying me. First, we would go to some fish place where there was singing and there were waitresses in black silk stockings and they made wonderful apple tart. It would be his treat.

We got there in good order, and the fish, the singing and the black silk stockings were all as promised. But the tart was off. By now Bill had drunk enough for any inadequacy or provocation to call for immediate retribution. Nothing on earth would stop him from sending for the head waiter, the manager, the proprietor, the landlord. He himself had declined the fish and the tart, saying he only wanted baked beans, which of course they did not have. Then he demanded *one* Brussels sprout, which, when produced, he ignored. As a consequence of this turbulence the dinner took a long time, and the situation was not enhanced by Bill's efforts to pull the waitress's knickers down each time she leaned over.

At last we were ready, the account settled. It was now long past the Clinic's requested admission time, but despite my protest Bill insisted that he himself would explain the reasons when we arrived. I knew what that would be like. Still, we sought out a taxi and set off. I tried to persuade him to take the taxi on but he would have none of it, it was his responsibility to see me safely in.

Once he had stumbled out of the taxi, the cool air must have gone to his head, for he suddenly plunged forward, grasping the revolving doors at the entrance. Under his full weight they gave way, propelling him at some speed into the foyer. There he slid to a stop, apparently out to the world, his brown bowler at his side. Simultaneously, the lift doors opened and an elderly, much made-up patient gingerly emerged, to be confronted with what seemed to be a corpse. A stretcher had to be found, for Bill had struck his head and was unconscious.

He appeared a day or two later at my bedside, in full Arab dress. Most of the clinic's patients at that time were Arabs, whose retinues squatted silently in the corridors. Since the Arabs tended to be rich rather than poor and paid lavishly, they were well looked after. I expressed some trivial complaint about the service to Bill, whereupon, breathing fumes of gin, he took it upon himself to give the nurses a severe reprimand in phoney Anglo-Arabic. They appeared impressed, especially since he had claimed princely status. On one occasion when he was with me we were interrupted by a piercing yell from the corridor. It turned out to be an Iraqi Brigadier returning from an unsuccessful visit to the lavatory; he had been operated on for piles the day before and forbidden to have a motion for at least forty-eight hours. Now he was stranded and in distress. The Floor Sister came out and upbraided him for his disobedience. In pain though he was, the Brigadier, helped to his feet by Bill, himself in Arab dress, replied with some asperity, "My dear lady, it has been my habit, every day of my adult life, to go to the Mess at noon, drink three martinis, lunch, and then have a shit, and I'm not going to change my habits now". "Then you're a very naughty boy," the Sister replied, wagging a bony finger at him, "and if you don't obey my orders you won't get another shit for at least a week."

Bill's brown bowler: in the end it became part of him, like his checked, waisted suits, high-cut, lapelled waistcoats, elastic-sided boots. His suits were made in Newbury to a style and pattern of his father's, and he looked, with his neat beard and rather florid complexion, like a character out of Chekhov. On his bad days he could be taken for a bookmaker drowning his sorrows. There was an Edwardian courtliness to Bill's sober manner – and he was usually sober three weeks out of four – a bowing to ladies and a kissing of hands. He took to wearing a musky, extremely pervasive scent, which gave him a sweet, bear-like aroma. He tended to brush his rather fine hair straight back, not quite *en brosse*, but in the manner of an Italian tenor, like Tino Rossi. I never saw it remotely ruffled, not even when he had fallen over.

Bill was a highly professional, disciplined writer, who never failed, whether travelling, on holiday, or staying with friends, to do a morning's stint at his desk. He was oddly fixed in his views and his habits, but once he had attended to his work he was a relaxed and delightful companion. For one who listed his recreation in *Who's Who* as "Watching", he was almost priggishly uninterested in social gossip. What fascinated him was the observation of others, preferably from an invisible vantage point. He was deeply envious of the perch I had during that hot week in Paris. It was not only on people, though, that he turned his beady eye: animals figure largely in his stories, and their behaviour, as well as the behaviour of weather, is treated with a suitable seriousness.

An Edwardian rake, a Russian aristocrat, a doctor during the time of the Habsburg Empire, a successful turf accountant; there was something of all of these in Bill. He was happiest in bizarre circumstances, restless in conventional gatherings. Once, in Berlin, he found himself in a club to which only men with beards were admitted. He was delighted by the sight of immensely well-dressed Berliners waltzing together, wearing gold watch chains and spats.

His four travel books, of which *Grand Tour Today* and *Away to it All* were the last, are full of oddities, scraps of surreal dialogue, peculiar rituals, obscure views, weird bits of information. He saw places through unique Sansomish eyes, and nowhere was ever the same after he had described it. Surprisingly, for one so curious about the world in general, he showed no interest in the Americas or any tropical country. He adored sitting in the sun, but not outside Europe. I tried many times to get him to come to India with me, or to Southeast Asia, where I thought what went on in Bangkok, or Penang or Singapore, would take his fancy, but he was adamant. Turkey was as far as he would venture in that direction, though he did not mind how far north he travelled.

Not long before he died he gave a nineteenth-century German ball in Hamilton Terrace. Guests were obliged to speak German and to be dressed in the style of the period. I knew it would end in disaster so I didn't go. For Bill, none of it would have been any effort. He inhabited the period anyway, he loved dressing up, German wine, German music and the German language, and the odds were that he would have passed out before most of the guests had arrived.

His time as a writer will surely come again. He was the most lovable, as well as the most contrary, of friends, and no one who ever set eyes on him could ever have assumed he was ordinary.

My first journey abroad as cricket correspondent of the *Observer* was to Australia in the autumn of 1954. The book that I subsequently wrote on a thrilling series of Tests and six months of travel was the first of four – one more on Australia, one on the West Indies, one divided between South Africa and England – in which I tried to give the cricket a wider context, relating it to landscape, climate, politics and local life. No one had really tried to do this before; the cricket generally appeared to take place in a kind of vacuum. Neville Cardus had been a student of character as much as of technique, of music as much as of cricket, but he hadn't really the instincts of a traveller. Moreover, tied as he was to the schedules of daily journalism, he was much less free than I was. A bottle of wine and a concert were as much as Neville demanded of Australia. It was nevertheless true that no one who wrote about the game after him could remain unaffected by the brilliance of his imagery and his ability to dismantle a player's presence and personality and reconstitute them at the wicket.

Those four tours were gregarious, enjoyable affairs, the

labour of writing the books offset by the sunshine, the excitement of unfamiliar places and the making of new friends. Press boxes were entertaining places in those days and relations between journalists and players less uneasy than they seem to have become since. England never lost a series that I covered and that certainly helped to keep everything friendly.

In the summer of 1956 the Australians were in England and I drove about the country, mainly on secondary roads, trying to see it as if it were abroad. The Tests, dominated by Jim Laker's bowling, provided interest enough, and the attempt to write about England through a stranger's eyes led me to all kinds of places I would never otherwise have seen. Apart from the cricket it was a solitary, reflective time; I drove alone through all kinds of weather and stayed in small country pubs where I wrote up the day's journey. At the end of it I felt I had learned something about England and something about myself. Unlike my travelling in Australia, the Caribbean and South Africa, my four months of crossing and recrossing England had a seasonal quality to it. It had begun in late April with the trees round the beautiful amphitheatre at Arundel just coming into leaf and ended in early September at a rainy Hastings, with the seagulls flapping under the castle and the fishing boats drawn up high on the shingle.

One other book emerged from a late summer and autumn journey just preceding my engagement with the *Observer*. That was *The Bandit on the Billiard Table*, now just about to be reprinted for the second time. I had read D. H. Lawrence's *Sea and Sardinia* during a period of passionate involvement with Lawrence, but it was the Nelson connection that drew me there. As with *Time Was Away* and *The Gulf of Pleasure* I wanted to combine prose and poetry. *Letters from Iceland*, by Auden and MacNeice, had always been a favourite book and though I had no illusions about attempting something in that manner, I felt that there was another way in which prose and poetry could complement each other.

The book was commissioned by Derek Verschoyle who was also responsible, while at Michael Joseph, for the publication of my first Australian book. *The Bandit* was illustrated with photographs by the adventurous and voluble Greek photographer A. Costa, who had earlier accompanied Patrick Leigh Fermor round the Caribbean and taken the pictures for *The Traveller's Tree*. Costa, nut-brown and bald, bore a marked resemblance to both Pablo Picasso and the Iraqi politician Mossadeq.

He was an accomplished photographer, despite having a weakness for obscure aristocrats. It was usually only when his hope of finding an elusive *principessa* or ageing *contessa* had been abandoned that he would concentrate on the business in hand. Costa had little interest in photographing low life or illustrating social conditions, but his eventual pictures of coral fisherboys and Romanesque churches, of costumed peasants and epicene priests, of the rugged Sardinian landscape and its ancient monuments, enhanced the book. Not long afterwards, on one of the enterprising journeys that he undertook in search of winter sun, he had an unfortunate encounter with a camel. Thereafter his photographs were less in evidence. He kept a small house in Godfrey Street, from which he occasionally emerged in a raffish suit, but for most of the year he based himself in the hills behind Nice.

While at Michael Joseph, Derek Verschoyle had met Moyra Slater, whom I had known some years earlier as the wife of Humphrey Slater. Humphrey, a notable figure in the International Brigade and editor of the magazine *Polemic*, which had a brief run after *Horizon* had folded, wrote a number of novels, the most successful of which, *Conspirator*, was made into a film with Elizabeth Taylor. Shortly afterwards, Humphrey died. Moyra had money of her own, and when she and Derek married she joined the recently founded publishing firm of Derek Verschoyle in Park Place, St James's. During its short life the firm produced a number of interesting books –

by, among others, Lawrence Durrell, Roy Fuller, Patrick Leigh Fermor, Denis Johnston, Christopher Sykes and John Marks – but Derek's ideas tended to run ahead of his capacity to deal with them. In no time huge losses had been run up, the scale of them concealed from Derek's other partners. When, in due course, these had to be confessed, further support was withdrawn and the firm went into liquidation. Derek rather sadly ended his days as editor of *The Grower*, and Moyra eventually disposed of him too.

In his pomp Derek was something of a figure, an entertaining fantasist with as little concern for the truth as his friend and contemporary Goronwy Rees. Even balder than Costa, with a pinkish complexion, Derek was dapper in appearance, though slightly moist and shifty about the eyes. He had numerous wives before Moyra and most of the marriages ended acrimoniously.

The Verschoyles came from County Sligo, and Derek went to Trinity College, Dublin, after leaving Malvern. A spell in Paris was followed by eight years, 1932–40, as literary editor of the *Spectator*, during which time he became friendly with Graham Greene, Peter Fleming and other regular contributors to the paper. He was, by all accounts, unpredictable but lively at his job, an impresario rather than a journalist by nature.

Goronwy Rees was, in 1936, assistant editor of the *Spectator*, which presumably was when the two of them met. I lost count in later years of the number of plays and books of memoirs Derek claimed to have just finished, but since none of them ever saw the light of day I doubt whether he wrote a word. The gin bottle used to come out at an early hour, so I imagine Derek belonged in the company of those who took the wish for the deed.

Throughout the war Derek served in some branch of Intelligence, nominally attached to the RAF, in which he attained the rank of Wing Commander. Goronwy Rees, who said on various occasions that he had made notes about Derek over many years for a memoir (alas, never written), told me an interesting wartime story. Considering Goronwy's own inventive powers there is no knowing whether it was true. According to Goronwy, Derek, who had been running a partisan unit towards the end of the war from Rome, was in the habit of requesting sums of money for the payment of a particularly successful agent. The information this agent was relaying via Derek to London had turned out to be so valuable that not only was the money authorized but, unknown to Derek, a senior officer was dispatched from London to interrogate and congratulate the man concerned. The "senior officer", Goronwy confided with wolfish glee, was himself. When he got to Rome and began to make inquiries it became clear that no such person existed. Derek had invented him, passing information based on his own inspired guesses.

When the war ended Derek was appointed First Secretary at the British Embassy in Rome, where he soon got involved with the wife of a fellow diplomat. The marriage that ensued ended the most violently of all. I never myself saw Derek in a rage; his outbursts were perhaps reserved for women. But, possibly as a result of an excess of gin, he sometimes looked as if he might explode, his face getting pinker and pinker, his eyes smaller. Although he liked to promote and receive gossip, Derek was not an easy talker. Sometimes he would invite me to lunch at the Garrick and find himself with nothing to say. I assume that on those occasions his general deviousness or marital problems were weighing heavily.

He was a considerate, genial, generous host, always delighted to purvey information of a kind not ordinarily come by. In this sense he was the reverse of a spy, but with similar instincts for elaborate fabrication. He put me up for the Garrick, seconded by my subsequent publisher – after the collapse of Derek's firm – Hamish Hamilton. At least it meant Derek would no longer always have to pay for my lunch.

The two men made an interesting contrast. Whereas Derek was always unrealistically optimistic about publishing projects – he wanted good things to succeed and unfortunately pretended that they had when they hadn't – Jamie Hamilton was exactly the opposite. Even when faced with incontrovertible evidence to the contrary he liked to make his authors feel that they, personally, were bankrupting him.

In fact, the firm was well and economically run, Jamie's social contacts and entrepreneurial skills ensuring a steady flow of celebrities, actors, musicians and socialites, as well as best-selling authors such as Nancy Mitford, Alan Moorehead, Georges Simenon and L. P. Hartley. Shortly before his death Leslie Hartley was made a Companion of Literature by the Royal Society of Literature, at the hands of R. A. Butler, and his fellow recipient was Cyril Connolly. I cannot remember a more farcical occasion. Butler, curiously inept and seeming almost gaga, referred to Connolly as a well-known novelist and had nothing to say about Hartley except that there was a racehorse called The Go-Between which he himself had once successfully backed. It was a sprinter, as a matter of fact, and won several races off the reel, the profits from which I also shared. On hearing his name called, Hartley, in a state of some confusion not unusual in his later years, made off from the throng in the wrong direction, ending up in the lavatory. Eventually extricated, he was guided towards Butler, but mistaking the scroll of honour in Butler's hands for a charitable request or some petition he was being asked to sign, began scrabbling for his chequebook and pen.

Jamie Hamilton had started his publishing life as the London Manager of the American firm of Harper. When, after five years of this, he decided to start his own firm in 1931, he was able to bring to it a number of successful American novelists and political commentators. During the '20s Jamie had been a distinguished oarsman, stroking winning crews in the Grand Challenge Cup at Henley and gaining a silver medal at the 1928 Amsterdam Olympics. There can rarely have been a man who wore his age better; in his seventies he was a more sprightly figure on the tennis and squash courts than most people thirty years his junior. He, as much as anyone, was part of London club life, of the Garrick in particular, until his Italian wife Yvonne hauled him into Florentine exile on his reluctant retirement.

The firm of Hamish Hamilton published two of my cricket books, *Cape Summer* and *Through the Caribbean*, a volume of poems called *To Whom It May Concern* and three stories for children, which I wrote to amuse my son when he was small. The drawings for the first two stories were done by a then unknown protégé of Max Martyn, the production manager. His name was Raymond Briggs and he soon became a neighbour, living along the lane from us in Sussex. When in 1965 I started my own publishing firm he illustrated the third of my children's books. His drawings had charm and style. In due course he sensibly decided he could write his own books as well as illustrate them. The results were ferocious and successful; with his ability to invent memorable characters and put them unflinchingly in settings not customarily deemed suitable for children, he created a genre entirely his own. There was an idea at one time for a film to be made of *The Onion Man*, the first of my books that Raymond illustrated, but like many schemes initiated by John Sutro it never materialized. In this instance it was scarcely John's fault, for the distinguished director assigned to the job took to the bottle and disappeared into a home for the next decade.

If the 1950s were the beginning of my time as a writer on cricket, a period which also produced travel books and volumes of poems, they were also years in which I made new and lasting friendships. Only Roy Fuller, as close as most to me, was a friend surviving from the war itself, but apart from those

with whom I had a professional relationship of some kind –
publishers, fellow writers and journalists – there were others
with whom I had the war in common but met later. Jeremy
Hutchinson, then married to Peggy Ashcroft, was one, Martyn
Beckett another. Jeremy I first met through Pam and Freddie
Mayor, whose gallery was one of the jolliest places in London.
Jeremy was brought up in Sussex and he, more than anyone
I knew, shared my passion for Sussex cricket. There has never
been a summer since 1955 when we have not watched Sussex
together at Hove or Lord's, euphorically happy or plunged
into gloom by a typical Sussex collapse. Soon after we moved
to Sussex the Hutchinsons acquired a ravishing downland
cottage conveniently placed for both Hove and Eastbourne.
George Cox, when he retired from first-class cricket, lived
nearby in Ditchling, and since both Jeremy and I had been
brought up on the Sussex cricketers of the '30s George's
comical, generous and enlivening presence, as well as the
lavish picnics provided by his wife Bette, added greatly to our
pleasure.

Jeremy, who like me had begun his war service as an
ordinary seaman, survived, just, the hazard of being in a
destroyer commanded by Mountbatten and ended up as a
lieutenant commander. The dangers of serving with
Mountbatten made his subsequent ordeals at the Old Bailey,
defending one notorious criminal after another, seem small
beer. Martyn Beckett in contrast, a wartime tank commander
and a Yorkshireman, could scarcely be expected to share our
addiction to goings-on at Hove, and when Yorkshire came
south there was some rivalry between us. Martyn, who plays
blues and jazz classics on the piano considerably more recog-
nizably than Bill Sansom, spent much of August, when we
were at Hove, on the grouse moors; his shooting skills, like
Ranji's, were renowned. Soon after I took over the *London
Magazine* Martyn set up on his own as an architect in South
Kensington, subletting two rooms to me, so that for twenty-one

years we worked in the same house. It was the greatest good luck.

I found one other new friend about now, who shared my interest not only in war and Sussex cricket but in poetry too.

This was Bernard Gutteridge, who had a cottage at Graffham in West Sussex. After a stormy marriage to a lively but unpredictable Egyptian, which produced the beautiful actress Lucy Gutteridge, Bernard had settled with a new wife into a large, shabby flat in Queen's Gate. When I first met him, Bernard was with J. Walter Thompson as a senior copy-writer who had got almost to the top. "Almost" was a signifi-cant word in regard to Bernard, who was prone to accidents, some of them brought on by alcohol not sufficiently absorbed. When his firm was taken over by Americans he measured his length in the act of being introduced to the new boss. So excessively forward a move did not enhance his standing with the transatlantic management.

Bernard had begun the war as a private in what is now the Royal Hampshire Regiment. He ended it as a major, G2 in 36 Division, in Burma, having got there by way of Madagascar and India. He served under all sorts of illustrious commanders, Mountbatten and Slim among them. He was very proud of this reflected celebrity and for as long as I knew him he claimed to be working on a book of military memoirs. Some fifteen years before he died, aged sixty-nine in 1985, he confided to me at Lord's one afternoon that the last chapter was being typed. He repeated this at increasingly long intervals but no one, I fear, ever saw a line of it. Either it only existed in his head or he had been associated with it so long he could not bear to part with it. There was a touch of the Verschoyle in him.

What did not only exist in his head was his poetry. He had produced several fine short poems during the war, mainly set

129

in Africa and Burma, and thirty years later, in *Old Damson Face*, which London Magazine Editions published in 1975, he wrote equally tersely and well about love and death, soldiering and sorrow, desire and drink. Drink was very much a part of Bernard, both in its convivial and its punishing aspect, and he wrote as persuasively and truthfully about it as anyone I know.

> The guest house, alcohol,
> Where you stay and are stayed.
> The drummer on the beach, the drum,
> The sticks, the taps,
> Old bruised legs along
> The empty promenade.
> Landlady of my gin!
> O Lodger whisky!

In appearance he was faintly Dickensian, balding, eyes moistly beaming behind round specs, pink-faced, spare. He wore bright, striped shirts, often with a bow tie, and he exuded good humour and comradeship. He told long, rambling anecdotes with infectious enthusiasm and was, in his gentle way, an amorist as well as a casual dandy.

In his copywriting heyday Bernard several times arranged large lunches, the ostensible purpose of which was to get advertising for the *London Magazine*, which I had begun to edit in 1961. To this end he invited directors of various agencies, MPs, businessmen, a tycoon or two. Not a quarter-page of advertising resulted from these gatherings but they were entertaining affairs and Bernard was in his element.

Bernard never drove, for understandable reasons, so in the country he was immobilized. I sometimes used to drive over and take him to Fontwell races, but generally we met in London. He liked to go to Lord's or to give lunches at Queen's Gate when there was a Test Match on the television. It was ironic that it was not Bernard, the great faller-over, who should have died in this fashion, but his second wife, Anne, who got up in the middle of the night and lost her footing on the tricky stairs down to the bathroom.

Bernard was an unusual drinker. He would be sitting happily beside you in a restaurant or a bar, seeming to have drunk nothing very much. Then, when it was time to go, he would turn rather guiltily and say, "I'm sorry, my dear, but I'm not going to be able to get up." Nor could he. He would have to be carried out. Still, if alcohol occasionally got the better of him, he made it work for him too. He never shrank from the truth.

> My Bar, "Good Morning" friend: damson face
> My looking-glass of fractured capillaries
> I shall hang up before me in a decade.
> That puffed nose you own will be mine;
> The hanging cheeks – such fritillaries –
> Shaking, shaking, shaking like the wine.

I don't think this leglessness can have afflicted him during his army days, for Bernard was obviously an efficient as well as a delightful soldier, of the kind that goes a long way towards making up for the tedium and the terror. Bernard's war poems were first published in 1947 under the title *Traveller's Eye*. They were, in fact, rather more to do with places – Mongmit, Tananarive, Mandalay, Shillong – than with military life or battle, but under their vivid, descriptive exterior there were haunted silences. His *Burma Diary* was an exception, a poem of over forty verses that, though set evocatively in such places as Arakan, Namma, Hopin and Myitson, quite deliberately contrasts the exoticism of the scenery with the quick, dry finality of death, when

> All that remains are the frailest moments
> Between two bursts: minute that is a friend gone,
> That is the twist of terror, a ricochet,
> A cloud, a sampan sinking.

In the same poem Bernard wrote, in his customary fatalistic manner:

131

So when I heard these last two afternoons
My friend, a poet, had died on the Goppe Pass;
Another, my dearest friend, next day was killed
    Leading his company –

And looking Eastwards to the Mayu Range,
Its barren hulk all burned up in the heat,
Somehow it was quite expected; and I write
    These arid lines, alive myself,

For the actual and real is Burma. Alun and Amyas
Will never return through the streams and jungle,
Their physical part of the pattern is ended . . .

Reading his poems again now I am more struck by their sadness and by his preoccupation with the dead than I was at the time. In "Gold Mohur" the last verse reads:

    You dead, my friends, still stay
    Like this exquisite tree
    My eyes must leave, heraldic
    Flowering I will not see
    Scald in April with crimson
    Showers of petals. Then lie
    There among its roots and blossom.
    Your graces to the moonstone sky
    It will yearly repay.

Perhaps there was in Bernard an underlying gentle melancholy that his generally genial exterior belied.

Latterly, he would bring his reviews for the magazine into our Thurloe Place office by hand. The stairs to the top were exacting for one not particularly fit, as Julian Maclaren-Ross often found, and by the time he appeared, very much the country gentleman up from Sussex for the day, Bernard was usually sweating and shaky. "I'll just sit down for a moment, my dear," he'd say, and he would be there an hour later, happy as a bird, discussing the team for the Test Match.

Fragile and rickety as he often appeared in London, so that

one feared for him when he crossed roads, in Sussex he had an altogether more robust character. Cloth cap on his head and stick in hand he would stride over the Downs and along country lanes for hours. There he really was the countryman he paraded in London, a lover of pubs and saloon-bar small talk, of village gossip and seasonal disasters.

He wrote curiously little about the country, much as he loved it. As his talk grew more rambling his poems grew more elliptical, with a rather bitter edge to them. His two sequences *Mother Goose* and *At the Lion* suggested, in poem after poem, a man tethered or trapped, sometimes by alcohol or a woman, more often simply by life:

> Under his seat, the battered
> Sealyham like his wife;
> The lead creaks as he jerks its
> Collar and tries to pretend
> To pretend to strangle his life . . .

and again, in a section of *At the Lion* called "My Life":

> She nags her life out of me.
> Over my whisky I see the poor sod run
> Shouting *bitch* over his shoulder.
>
> And here she comes back out of the Ladies,
> Dribbling it back at me,
> Preparing to shoot.

In one of his very last poems he describes a wedding:

> Notice the young lady breaking
> The bottle, naming the ship Venture.
> Remember that at each wedding,
> Each launching,
> Mutiny is the first stowaway.

Bernard, I think, was fortunate in his friends, but unfortunate in his women, who tended to be domineering or unfaithful, and with more of a taste for alcohol than was wise in a companion for him. When, during the last few years of his life, he was alone and without a London base, he appeared less victimized, if also more vulnerable.

Bernard went suddenly and too soon, like that other equally engaging and talented Bernard, Bernard Spencer, whose poems I had so long and so much admired and which – alas, after his death in Vienna, where he fell mysteriously out of a train – I was later to put in my first list as a publisher.

Bernard Gutteridge had no business dying when he did and it seems to have been at least partly through neglect. I remember him coming into the office some months before he died and remarking that he had been having difficulty swallowing. His country doctor had told him not to worry, it was an affliction common among those getting on a bit. Then, out of the blue, a postcard arrived, addressed from the Royal Free Hospital in Hampstead, saying he was going to have an exploratory operation on his throat and would be out of action for a week or two. He had just done a review for us of Philip Ziegler's *Mountbatten* and I must have suggested something else he might like to do.

He had his exploratory operation and then another one, from which he scarcely regained consciousness. Had cancer been diagnosed when he first reported his symptoms he might well be still alive.

Mongoose

Half-squirrel, half-rat, but with the incisors
Of the real killer, he has come
Into his own silk empire. In naves
Of cool cane he basks like a voluptuary,
Savouring his whiskers. He is in charge now,
Wet-mouthed addict from whom, like the cutters,

Africa is remote, a mere rolling of eyes.
They have won through together,
Shedding their serfdom. Thus do we see them,
Plush overseers on the crown of the road,
Those nights when we cruise through molasses,
Our headlamps spraying long grasses
That sometimes are set fire to. Homeless,
Then, these rodent police, eyes like paraffin,
Scuttle before us, their empire in flames.

Mayaro

Between Manzanilla and Mayaro
The beach runs straight as a ruler.
You can drive a car on it.
The Atlantic comes in on foam curlers,
And between them and the crocodile river
Royal palms are as splendid as Nubians.

We have hauled up hundreds
Of chip-chips, silvery bivalves the sun polishes.
All morning we swam among Indians on bicycles,
Lying out in the shade of a hotel
Going bankrupt. The forest encroaches,
Tying up balconies with festooning liana.

Rock Paintings, Drakensberg

These mountains of up-pointed spears
Hold eland, oribi and rhebok
Capering over yellow rock
To sandstone caves that form a barrier

Eastward mauve and vertical,
Westward greenly gradual.
Sweet grasses swish below like silk
Torn at dark by prowling buck.

Baboons on red and scrabbling paths
Scatter dust in layers of talc,
Imitating as they stalk
Human gestures, hurling oaths.

A form of sympathetic magic
More good-natured now than tragic,
Though practised by the bushman hunter,
Re-creating as a painter

Animals he hoped to capture,
Art was not a surplus rapture,
But a means of softening up
Hartebeest and antelope.

Here walls of cave and sky converge;
Within, the human primal urge.
Brush-pigs scuttle from cracked rocks,
Bush-girls thrust their weighted buttocks

Squatting as they chant in line
Round pots of boiling porcupine.
The painted bushman aims his bow,
The real sunset starts to flow

Across this sweeping mountain range
And still, despite ten centuries' change,
Art remains a kind of hunt
Eliminating fear and cant,

A means of pinning down
An object, by the sheer act
Of drawing animal or loved one,
Making absence into fact.

Bus Boycott

Two hours walk to work and back.
Rolling their eyes and rolling slightly,
Loose as runners on running tracks,
At dawn setting off, they return nightly
To where their shanty chimneys thrust
Blackened funnels from roofs of rust.
Over the saffron, smoke-smeared veld,
Braziers gleaming in mauve-pink hollows,
Alexandra township's dust
Settles, as trilbies tilted, collars
Sodden, they slow up on the journey back.

Eight miles there and eight miles back.
Such exercise is beneficial,
Medical evidence is official
– though two hours walk on Kaffir beer,
Belching as the fortunate steer
Unsteady routes through blackleg cars
Offering lifts and opening doors
Usually closed, needs a clear
Motive to sustain the miles
Wearing down the twisted smiles.
Shoes in hand to save the leather,
At least they're certain of the weather
On the journey there and journey back.

Two hours there and two hours back.
Buses idle in their hangars,
Illustrate their only right,
To withhold custom from the white.
A penny busfare raise has proved
The straw upon the camel's back.
At checkpoints, passes are demanded,
Holding them up along the track
Of this ballooning dream that severs
Economic links that bind

The victim to his servile grind.
Today will never be countermanded,
There cannot be a journey back.

Two hours there, and two hours back.
The glinting corrugated iron
Beckons in its smoking bowl,
Smells of mealie, smells of fear,
Which pedestrian workers share
With tsotsis on their evening prowl
For retribution – an apprehension lying
Like thunder in the sinking air.
Sweating sourly, each relying
On a corporative idea,
Follows his nose, and follows freely
His instinct there, his instinct back.

Secretary Bird

Its name describes it, even to those penholder patches
Behind pale ears, the desiccated manner, head tilted
Back, offended, supercilious as it scratches
The scrub for snakes, faltering on stork-stilted
Legs feathered grey-black with sore patches.

No other name could so well have drawn
Forth the image, as I saw it, near Philippolis, alone
Among thornbushes, in the red earth sharp stones
And waterwheels glinting, but in the whole Karoo
Only it moving, abstracted, wondering what to do.

Since Kroonstad, 500 miles back, nothing so human
Had stirred in the desert, no man nor carrying woman,
So that stopping my car I had jumped it nearer
Through glasses, as on inadequate legs it came clearer,
Uncertainly swerving, as if blown by the dust.

Something about that haphazard swerve must
Have caught my memory, jolting me suddenly back
To a sailboat of a girl, quite incongruously unlike
It, but who moved so – indelibly so –
Through a part of my life, a few years ago.
I smiled at the absurdity, to find, as I let
In the clutch, my eyes unaccountably wet.

In Bloemfontein

Woman to man, they lie,
He not quite white
As she, nor she
So black as he.

Save where her stomach curves
His flesh and hers,
Commingling, match.
Eyes catch,

That dare not meet
Beyond the night,
Though their alternate
Thighs, locked tight,

Defy you to discriminate
Between his skin and hers.
To him Pass Laws
Apply; she knows no night.

But that pale stripe her loins
Keep from the sun
Marks her, his tiger-woman,
White, while he's all one.

That stripe convicts. He covers
With his hand the site
Of crime. Soon shutters,
Striping him with light,

Peel colour from his hips –
She his woman, he
Her man, simply human
Like the heart beneath her lips.

A matter of degree
Elsewhere, no more;
But here, in Bloemfontein,
Keep closed the door.

Sundown, Natal

Sea smoked like salmon,
As over hills of almond,
Blond rinds of sand,
The sun past Amanzimtoti dips –
That precise shade her lips
Take on when neon-lit,

Or the soles of a negress's feet.

Dandy in Eloff Street

With fawn fedora and a rolled umbrella,
Palm Beach suit and co-respondent shoes,
He eyes himself in dummy-grinning windows,
Smiling when his image in the plate-glass does.

Creases sharp as razors, but avoiding ladders,
He prowls up Eloff on a short-term shadow.
His teeth are gleaming and his tie is yellow.
The outer man on show, the inner one lies fallow.

Arrogant in his fancies, building castles
In the air, he scrutinizes fingernails and whistles
Softly to himself (as if all that matters
Is precisely how much cuff exceeds the sleeve).
Behind smoked lenses, his bloodshot eyes are eagles,
Swooping insults up from looks of alleged betters.
His nostrils sniff out scorn, and, flaring, leave
A trail of wounded self-love like a spoor.

Chest puffed out, a nylon pigeon, his lips are bugles
Blowing fanfares of his pride from door to door.
Yet, salesman of himself in imaginary encounters,
Randy dandy on the loose from rancid shanties,
He wears out self-respect, overdrawing by instalments,
Spiritually bankrupt, though a strolling millionaire.
At home, the suit hangs up, still bluffing its contentment.
Its owner sags: the dandy is up there.

Assiut Station

Along this single-line track – the Nile
Spiked with palm fins – midnight and milling crowds
Await the Cairo Express. Breathing fire
And thunder, never stopping for them,
It fillets the darkness, disperses interest.

At the station, where Nasser looks down
From huge posters and examples of Soviet art
Decorate the platforms, now it's gone

Horse-carriages clop quietly away
Past the fountain, down the one street.

But something of Old Russia
Survives, exuded from the pores
Of an army of putty-faced technicians,
Here like ourselves almost by chance,
Drinking mint tea, playing backgammon

– Nothing in common between any of us,
Exchanging not even a glance.

Sunset at Edfu

A sunset at first so pale it's hardly there –
Merely a suffusion of pink over sandstone,
A faint flushing of the wake –
Then the egrets, as exact in formation
As Spitfires, turn their wings all colours.
Felucca sails stain gold, hulls black.

Soon curiously it's all in reverse –
Orange, lavender, peppermint, like wash
Transfers on the sand, as if linen
Were laid there to dry. And in midstream
Watching through binoculars the herons totter,
We catch on the breeze whiffs of molasses.

At this hour silence wraps
Up the river, squeezing the last drops
From what here is the only
Benevolence of nature, the tried god –
A sun slipping over the desert like ice
Leaving a rim pink as lipstick on a glass.

A Crow in Rhodes

Dilapidated Greek crow, subfusc
And shabby below the morning glories,
Astride the banana leaves or tittuping
Like a half-pissed lawyer between jacaranda
And frangipani, bougainvillea and plumbago,
You simulate great age, wreak
Private havoc with your black secateur.

Penitent in your tailcoat, venerable
Dud waiter or clerk in failing chambers,
That shutter of an eye, flickery
As *cinéma bleu*, makes baleful apology
For a morning of shit and extravagance.
What you haven't knocked off bears
No mentioning. You're in your element, old gammy-leg.

You're one of the family now, alert
For privileges (and don't you show it),
Blasphemous as a bootlegger at breakfast,
Stumping around all day, ham-
Acting your injury while the rest of us, stunned
By the heat, marvel at your energy –
There's no holding you, ancient old astronaut.

Yet it's barely a week since,
More dead than alive, you fell
Limp as a shuttlecock on to our terrace,
Victim of overconfidence but certain
Of immortal properties, a special claim
On our sympathy. From a death
To a myth so soon is good going,
Old walking-wounded, old scabface.
Now earn your keep with this poem.

PART IV

North Africa

THERE IS A POEM of Bernard Gutteridge's which reads:

> Bottle tops fall always upside down.
> Crown-corks they are called in the trade.
> Foliated, crimped,
> When done with there's a dent in them
> Like all us gentlemen.

Few of us are not dented, one way or another, by the time we reach middle age. This was certainly true of John Gale, the dent in whom was responsible for a brief but abrupt change in my winter routine. My summers, throughout the years 1950–72, were more or less given over to the *Observer*, but during the winter, except when MCC were touring – in those days to Australia every four years, to the West Indies and South Africa every eight – I was fairly free. I had to do occasional pieces for the *Observer*, but otherwise I spent my time translating and reviewing books and trying to write poetry. After 1961 everything changed, because from then on I had the *London Magazine* to look after.

One day in March 1958 I received a message that the editor of the *Observer*, David Astor, would like to see me, rather urgently. Michael Davie, who had been in the XI with me during my last summer at Haileybury, was then working in some capacity at the foreign news desk, and Mark Arnold-Forster, whom I had known when he was an exceptionally dashing MTB captain at Felixstowe in 1944, was foreign editor. In due course Michael Davie became sports editor, then assistant editor, before going off to Australia to edit the *Age* in Melbourne.

On this particular afternoon a crisis had arisen. John Gale, the paper's correspondent in Paris, and before that in Algeria, had apparently gone off his head. "We'd like you to go to North Africa for us," David Astor said. "John Gale's been behaving very oddly lately and I think he's ill. He has the illusion he's being followed by the Paras and that people are putting drugs in his drinks."

Whether any of this was true – and just conceivably some of it was, because John, by his passionate condemnation of French policy in Algeria, had made himself very unpopular with certain people in France – John had now become extremely disturbed and paranoid. He had begun to equate what the French paratroops were doing in Algeria with what the Germans had done in France and elsewhere during the war. There was a particular parachute battalion of the Foreign Legion, the Green Berets, many of whose members were German and some ex-SS, who were renowned for the refinements of their torture. During John's time covering the Algerian war people were tortured and shot daily, simply disappeared or committed suicide. For one of John's temperament, highly imaginative and sensitive, prone to violent swings of mood and to taking things too much to heart, it was a demoralizing experience. In the book that he wrote about his eventual crack-up, *Clean Young Englishman*, he quotes his wife, Jill, saying to him, "Why can't you be more natural and take things in a straightforward way?"

Natural was something John never quite managed to be. He complains in his book about his emotional coldness, an inability to play his full part in a relationship, but he came over to friends as someone only too highly charged: boisterous, teasing, high-spirited. Yet, under a boyish, innocent sort of manner, there was a nervous edge to him.

John was three years younger than I was and so most things that happened to us -- in his case Stowe, the Coldstream Guards, journalism – happened to him just that much later. I think, nevertheless, we must have more or less coincided on the *Observer*, at one of its great periods, when people like Patrick O'Donovan, Kenneth Tynan, Hugh Massingham, John Pringle, Harold Nicolson and Penelope Gilliatt were all writing for it. But whereas I never had to work on the premises, John, though often abroad, was very much part of the daily life of the paper.

He had not made an auspicious start to his career. In his first job as a general reporter on a Midlands paper he had managed to get the magistrate on probation instead of the offender in a court story. He moved to the *Sunday Express* but soon, in common with several others at the time of the news-print shortage, got the sack. He was kept going by his wife, a ballet dancer working at that time in a nightclub.

The *Observer* job was the break he needed. He progressed from defending suede shoes, reporting strikes and covering odd stories to becoming the paper's Cairo correspondent at the time of Suez. When he was in London he turned out sometimes for the *Observer*'s cricket team, whose more stalwart members were telephonists, messengers and administrative staff rather than journalists. John was not only good-looking in a fair-haired, Guards-officer kind of way; he was also physically strong and competitive. He pretended not to take anything seriously, questioning every accepted viewpoint and aspect of behaviour, but in fact he did, rather too much for his own health. He was one of those people, too, who saw both sides of every issue. Typically, he observed in *Clean Young Englishman*: "I shall never forget the humanity of the Egyptians throughout the Suez affair."

The Algerian war had been going on for almost three years

when John was sent there in the summer of 1957. General Massu, a great brute of a man, was commanding the parachute division in Algiers. It was as well, at the time of John's initial interview with him, that neither knew much about the other. They were to learn soon enough.

Within weeks of John's arrival two thousand heavily-armed French troops, with tank and air support, had surrounded a couple of hundred Algerians, armed only with ancient rifles. All but five of the Algerians were killed in a battle lasting forty-eight hours. The five survivors were tied back to back in a truck and paraded through the streets of Tebessa while loudspeakers played "Madelon".

After a few months reporting such incidents – and that battle was one of the mildest cases of brutality then prevalent in Algeria – John was recalled to London and redirected to Paris. At the time assassinations were commonplace there; of Algerians by other Algerians, of Frenchmen who opposed the war, of liberals sickened by the bloodlust of the French right wing. It was while he was in Paris, working on profiles of Biaggi, leader of the newly-formed paramilitary Patriotic Revolutionary Party, and Robert Lacoste, the veteran socialist Minister Resident in Algeria, that John's delusions – if such they were – began. "I was drinking too much," he wrote. "I had begun to have an odd, fuzzy feeling in my feet." Next came the conviction he was being followed, that his coffee was being drugged.

Although he was clearly ill, John's real breakdown did not surface until later. He was given less challenging tasks, such as covering CND's first Aldermaston march. A few months later, when de Gaulle had ousted Soustelle, John flew to Tunis where the FLN had their headquarters. He wrote back in a letter that he had danced in a cabaret with a beautiful blonde in black tights who disappointingly turned out to be a man. The paper sent him to Formosa, to cover the activities of the American Seventh Fleet.

As a result of what he wrote about Algeria John was invited by the State Department to visit the United States. It was during this period that his symptoms took a more alarming turn. He left a suitcase containing his passport and his type-writer in the middle of Los Angeles railway station because he wanted to get rid of them. In his new-found state of freedom – his money had gone too – he began to feel the walls of his hotel room in El Paso closing in on him. "They were out to get me," he told the psychiatrist summoned to give him clearance to fly home. He took to singing hymns and looking for microphones under beds and in radiators. He shouted at strangers for appearing to stare at him.

Back in London the fuzzy feeling in his feet returned. He began shouting at men in pubs to get rid of their hearing aids. Men in glasses came to seem sinister to him, conspirators in a plot to burn up the world. John spent his thirty-fourth birthday in the clinic to which he was eventually taken. He spent four painful months there, at first heavily drugged, and then given ECT. *Clean Young Englishman* ends with his discharge.

There were another fifteen years to be got through. Up to a point – the point that allowed him to function as a journalist but not to take on assignments of the old kind – John recovered. Instead of covering wars and crisis areas he was put to writing domestic features – interviews with eccentric characters or celebrities on a visit – that were not likely to raise his, or anyone else's, emotional temperature. He did these very well, in his own inimitable style.

After a few years of such work John was offered a job in Hong Kong. The *Observer* had connections there with an English language journal that carried features on Southeast Asia. It was a change, it offered scope for travel and it was not demanding. John accepted the job and took his family. While he was there I called him up and we went together to Macao. I had not long recovered from a crack-up of comparable severity to John's, though quite different in manifestation. I had spent some weeks travelling round India, Malaysia and Thailand before moving on to Hong Kong. Johnny seemed moderately content in a slightly doped, distracted sort of way.

He returned to England and the *Observer*. Then, one day in 1974, unable to face forever taking the drugs that kept him stable, he killed himself. He left behind an unrevised, semi-autobiographical novel, *Camera Man*, set mainly in Hong Kong. The principal character, torn between loyalty and a restless need for romance, shared most of John's problems and some of his experiences. He was disguised, rather thinly, as a photographer. As a book it reeks of John, since, whatever he wrote, he was incapable of not giving it the impress of his own strong but strangely innocent personality. A colleague on the *Observer*, John Heilpern, edited the book after John's death, and it was published five years later.

I approached John's crusading, anti-Para zeal with a faint scepticism at first, but I prepared myself for North Africa by reading his dispatches to the office and such other relevant stuff as I could lay my hands on. I had been attracted to Tunisia, where I would be based, ever since reading, during the war, Henry de Montherlant's *La Rose de Sable*, as well as Norman Douglas's *Fountains in the Sand* and André Gide's *Journals*. It was an attraction that had little to do with nomadic life or politics, but derived from a romantic image of oases. I had also recently come across a strange account of ghetto life in Tunis, *The Pillar of Salt* by Albert Memmi. From my reading I knew that, among other things, Tunisia was a cold country with a hot sun.

I flew to Tunis on a cold March day, my initial brief being to send back over the next few weeks reports on the situation of the Algerian refugees in Tunisia. The Tunisia Palace Hotel, where I lodged, was mainly given over to journalists; the majority were French, but there was also a scattering of representatives from leading European journals. The atmosphere was faintly *Scoop*-like, with conflicting rumours flying around and people disappearing off on unspecified missions. Others remained steadfastly attached to the bar, preferring to stay close to sources of official information on principle, or simply being lazy.

Every day a press conference was held. President Bourguiba himself gave frequent interviews or spoke on the radio denouncing the French. Bourguiba was curiously like a darker-skinned Charlie Chaplin to look at, with comparable gifts of mimicry and dramatic irony. Pictures of him stared at you from every hoarding, and it was incontestably his strong, mature and tolerant personality that gave this newly independent country its dignified image.

It was only three years earlier that Bourguiba, imprisoned and exiled at frequent intervals by the French, had led his Neo-Destour party to form the first government of independent Tunisia. What soon became plain as I moved around was that, to a greater degree than in most African or Middle Eastern countries, the remnants of the distant past dominated the present. The legacy of the Roman protectorate, which resulted from the defeat of Carthage, was vividly present in the surviving ruins of the then newly founded cities of Tabarka, Dougga and El Djem. Further back, the Phoenician cities of the ninth century BC – Carthage, Gabès, Sfax, Sousse and Bizerta – still survived as picturesque and integrated adornments to modern cities.

The Romans had begun the cultivation of wheat, olives and vines here, and when in turn Vandals, Byzantines and Arabs invaded the country, the old Tunisian cities simply took on another face, becoming the capitals of Muslim Africa. In 1881 the 300-year-old hereditary dynasty of the Deys and Beys was brought to an end by the arrival of the French, whose own 75-year period of influence was now coming to an end.

Stains from every century, like wine deposits, flavoured the city; medieval Muslim Tunis walled, tortuous and cool; modern European Tunis orderly, geometrical, dazzling. Wherever one looked buildings, whether sugary Turkish, gilded Byzantine, domed Moorish, or cubed French, echoed and elaborated the colours of sand and sea, desert and sky. On walls and ramparts, mosques and monumental stone gates, these colours, reinforced by salt white, were repeated as if no others existed. The veiled woman rolled up in her white bolt of material and the white-suited businessman walked under a sky that plunged its blue into the Lake of Tunis. The uniformed spahis on their white horses moved against a sky that seemed to be melting. Villa and palace, factory and shop, hotel and café, arranged their striped awnings or squares of white wall against this unyielding blue. Splayed, salt-coated palms, clusters of orange trees, the fruit glowing like light bulbs, rows of derricks along the harbour, red fezzes, merely emphasized and set off the dominance of blue and white.

Beyond the city, free of the suburbs, olive, almond and cherry radiated like the spokes of a wheel. Fields buttered with mimosa or smeared with daisies and violets alternated with stubby vines, and alongside green cylinders of wheat and asparagus, pears and peaches sprayed against low hills.

Writing nearly a century ago, Gide had lamented the building of the broad, tree-lined boulevards that characterize the modern city. "In the evening all the whites became mauve and the sky the colour of a tea-rose," he wrote, "in the morning the whites became pink against a faintly violet sky. But I missed the white, grave classical Tunis of the autumn. Trees are being planted in the side streets and in the squares. Tunis will be more charming because of them; yet nothing could disfigure it so much."

It is a point of view, but Tunis has grown becomingly into its Western foliage. The Place de l'Indépendence and the Avenue Habib Bourguiba, leading from the Medina to the harbour, are so roofed with double rows of palm and fig that the flower stalls lining them never leave the shade. These stalls, looped with circular wreaths like painted bicycle tyres, flavour and cool every square. Creamy arums, black orchids, irises, sheet-white stocks, form heavy-scented oases round which trams rattle and tiny Renault taxis dart like mice.

I spent a few days acquiring Press passes and transport, reading up official hand-outs and listening to Bourguiba's hypnotic broadcasts. In the evenings I dined in the hotel or at an excellent restaurant, Mon Village, where the food was better than the local Koudiat wines. I learned from an Italian colleague on the *Corriere della Sera* that the huge phallic pepper-pots in general use at the time were known among the foreign press as Rubirosas, named after the Dominican millionaire diplomat and playboy Porfirio Rubirosa, whose sexual conquests and capacities had earned him celebrity. The local brothel was patronized nightly by the same colleague but it was an unappetizing barrack-like place with the atmosphere of a public bath.

I set off as soon as I could for the refugee camp at Aïn-Khemouda. You came on it suddenly: a cluster of tents on a shallow hill overlooking a thin but fast-flowing *oued* about three hours' drive into the desert. The Algerian frontier, which ran due south from the coast following the line of the mountains, was ten miles to the west. It would have been easy to have missed the Camp, or to have driven by without giving it much thought, were it not for the flag with its red crescent fluttering from a pole among a heap of white stones above the highest of the khaki-green tents.

As we drove up, groups of turbaned old men, bearded and burnt brown, were leaning against rough parapets waiting for the Ramadan gun to end the day's fast. There was an agreeable smell of cooking, and smoke curled gently from the entrance of each tent. There were children about and one might have imagined the encampment to have been an unusually large gathering of nomadic shepherds.

The old men got to their feet on my approach, fumbling in their tattered robes for what at first looked like open wallets containing family photographs. In fact, they were identity cards; the French had accused them of being Tunisians and not Algerians at all. There was no need to question them, for each identity card bore the official stamp of the Department of Tebessa, the zone in which the Morice line ended. This line, 250 miles long and starting on the coast at Bône, consisted of electrified barbed-wire barriers between which armed French trains constantly patrolled. For most of its length the Morice line ran twenty to thirty miles inside the Algerian frontier, a mountainous corridor recently scorched at the instigation of Chaban-Delmas, the French Minister of Defence. It was through this rough, seemingly impenetrable strip that the Algerian refugees at Aïn Khemouda had somehow made their way.

The camp at Aïn-Khemouda, administered by Red Crescent and United Nations officials from the neighbouring towns of Sbeitla and Kasserine, held three thousand people when I was there. The FLN in Tunis boasted that they knew thirty-six methods of crossing the Morice line, but recently it had become impossible for women and children to escape.

I spent a day at Aïn-Khemouda, most of the time examining the identity cards so eagerly proffered. It was as if their verification was a first step towards confirmation of their owners' existence, a stage towards the putting down of new roots, somewhere, anywhere. Germany had been like this ten years earlier; people on the run with no homes and no possessions. Something like 60,000 Algerians had fled the country in the last three years and they were being added to daily, not in large numbers, but singly or in small groups, usually without family.

The faces of some of the refugees remain in my memory. For instance, that of Bach Djabi, whose card recorded him as *cultivateur*, the son of Mohamed and Khamsa Ben Ohmed, born in 1899 at Bekkaria. He stood stiffly in front of me holding the hand of his son, a huge-eyed child of six. He had arrived the night before, having hidden in the mountains by day and taken three nights over the crossing. A week earlier his wife, much younger than himself, had been raped by five men before his eyes and killed, together with his other two children. The old man and the small boy, representatives of a village that no longer existed, exuded the suffering of animals in their total dependence on others.

Each person in the camp, man or woman, had his or her story of rape, violation, torture. A beautiful girl of seventeen, the victim of a multiple rape days after giving birth, showed the milk still in her breasts; an old crone described her own rape and the electric treatment and buggery meted out to her husband for protesting. A handsome patriarchal figure, incongruously dressed in turban, knickerbockers and slippers, was swung from a beam with his hands tied above his head.

When you have heard dozens of such stories, and read about hundreds more, the scale of it ceases to have meaning. The people at Aïn-Khemouda were anxious to show their scars, but they did so quietly and with dignity. The worst torture, worse even than the electrocution of the testicles, was when the orifices of people's bodies were filled with water and they were stamped on.

The replies to the questions "Why were you tortured?" and "Why did you leave?" were always the same. "Because they said I was feeding the Fellagha and because they burned up my village." In most cases the torture was gratuitous, a warning rather than a punishment, because the Fellagha were up in the mountains and made only lightning raids. An old man who had lost his wife and four children said to me, "I never saw the Fellagha and I never helped them, but I would now,

157

and if I were younger I would go back across the frontier and give blow for blow."

I left the camp with the black eyes of a dirt-stained boy of four – the same age as my own son – following me, his only possession the absurdly large, double-breasted pepper-and-salt coat that someone had given him. He was childishly proud of it. It was all he had, apart from the label round his neck, which bore the name "Mohamed" and after it the words "no known surviving relatives". There was complaint in the French papers during this period that the Tunisians were using these camps for propaganda purposes and that they had no business meddling in Algerian affairs. It was not a view with which anyone who visited the camps could sympathize.

That night, in the cold dark of Kasserine, you could hear the sporadic firing of French guns. After witnessing the effect of the Algerian situation on the French, it was something of a relief to realize that Britain's colonial wars were over, and that bloodshed on the Algerian scale – a million lives in seven years – was unlikely ever again to take place in a British colony.

Strictly speaking, the Algerian war was a civil war, since in the French fashion Algeria, like Martinique, for example, had long been absorbed into metropolitan France. The three million French settlers in Algeria were, in any case, the largest single group in the country, a third of the total Muslim population.

At the time of my visit, de Gaulle was a few weeks short of returning to power. Shortly after I left, in May, he came back, supported by the Army and by the French settlers of the three Algerian departments. "*Algérie Française*" – the chanting of which would be a familiar sound in Paris and on our television news bulletins for months to come – was an inspiring banner for an old soldier to march to, but by this time it was no more than a holding process. Four years later, at Evian, the dream of Algerian independence was made a reality. The safeguards written in for the settlers were soon abandoned and they left *en masse*. The butchery and the violence had been for nothing. Only the bitterness remained.

Bizerta is just less than fifty miles north of Tunis, and during the years of the French presence it was an important naval base. The bars of the old city and the promenade cafés were a lively sight with the red pompons of the French sailors bobbing about like poppies. Fifteen years earlier I had served briefly as a liaison officer in the Free French destroyer *La Combattante*, and I still could not see a French sailor, despite the present alienation, without a feeling of complicity.

There were some to be seen at Bizerta, straggling along the corniche road on which I made frequent journeys. Although the French Navy was not viewed in the same light as the Paras, it had become, by association, representative of the enemy. France in 1958 may have retained the sympathy of ex-colonials and old India hands, familiar with the ambiguities of the settlers' cause, but to most people the behaviour of her army, and of the Paras in particular, had become insupportable. It was scarcely surprising, when Klaus Barbie came to be tried thirty years later, that his counsel's main argument was that, with their record in Algeria, the French were in no position to try a man for crimes against humanity.

Although Tunisia had acquired, under Bourguiba, complete independence, the French had retained some of their military installations here. At Bizerta there was now the incongruous situation of 15,000 armed Frenchmen, with numerous aircraft, two minelayers and considerable supplies of ammunition at their disposal, being confined behind barbed-wire entanglements – put up by themselves – while 400 poorly armed Tunisians surrounded them, nominally for their own safety. The recent bombing by the French Air Force of the small Tunisian village of Sakiet Sidi Youssef had created a wave of revulsion against the French, and French troops in Tunisia were obliged, for their own good, to stay out of sight. Only at night, in plain clothes, did they sometimes emerge. The Officers' Club was closed and the womenfolk doing their shopping were the only sign of their presence.

For the most part, though protracted negotiations were being carried on about the French aerodromes in the south – out of twenty-one airfields in Tunisia theoretically available to the Algerian rebels France had the use of only four – relations between the Tunisians and the French were scrupulously polite. The Algerian Fellagha had their own brand of ruthlessness, displayed to peasants who did not shelter or feed them, as much as to the *colons*, which did something to offset the brutal image of the Paras.

While I was in Bizerta, Bourguiba made a series of speeches in which he insisted on the principle of Tunisian sovereignty. Independence was not independence if he had no control over troop movements inside Tunisia nor over the use of naval bases and aerodromes. Nevertheless, these repeated requests for the evacuation of French troops were political rather than realistic gestures. Tunisia's dependence on France, in those days, was almost total. While Bourguiba was obliged to continue his token protests he carefully made no mention of the more important chain of French radar stations linking Bizerta to Djerba nor of the aircraft taking off at regular intervals from Karouba airfield to supply the French outposts in the south.

The longer I was in the country the more the whole situation between Tunisia and France came to resemble a shadow play – the puppets went on making threatening faces but took care not to give each other a real whack. Each side, standing on principle, and having to be seen to stand on principle – the Tunisians on the issue of sovereignty, the French on military agreements – had to make do with the discussion of irrelevant details. The actual value to the French of Bizerta was minimal, at least as far as the war in Algeria was concerned, and though Bourguiba was obliged, for obvious political reasons, to make complaining noises about French intrusiveness, they were not, by either country, to be taken seriously.

There were roadblocks all over Tunisia, but between Tunis and Bizerta there were twice as many as anywhere else. These consisted of rough walls of stones not quite meeting across the road and a few sandbags. Desultory figures in the familiar brown-and-white striped woollen hoods acted as overseers, while a Neo-Destour soldier with a sub-machine-gun loafed in the vicinity. The roadblocks had no practical function whatsoever. They were simply one more form of war game, their purpose being to utilize manpower and symbolize the gravity of the situation.

I called on the Tunisian governor of the port one afternoon. The Tunisians had put a boom across the entrance to the harbour, which, had the French ships wished to leave, could have been removed as easily as if it had been a piece of seaweed. The Governor was absent from his office, but in the process of trying to establish whether any of my shipmates in *La Combattante* happened to be in the port, I remarked to an aide on the quietness of the day. I meant in relation to the storms and rain of the previous week, but mistaking me he put on a surprised and hurt face. "And why shouldn't it be quiet?" he said. "We lead quiet lives here. Everything is under control."

Back in Tunis I listened to Bourguiba outlining a plan for neutral control of the Algerian frontier. The idea was firmly rejected by the French Government. The day before, the French had proposed that neutral observers should be posted along the frontier to stop Tunisian aid to the rebels. This Bourguiba had rejected. And so it went on.

After a month in Tunis I made plans to travel south. The suburbs of Salammbo and Carthage, with caramel-headed children running in and out of blinding-white columns as if it were a bomb site; the beaches of Gammarth and Hammamet, the latter a notorious haunt of wealthy homosexuals; the Roman ruins at Dougga; the picture-postcard hill village of Sidi Bou Said – all these were within easy reach of the city. I drove out through olive groves and past salt-marshes to Enfidaville, a pilgrimage in memory of Keith Douglas, four of whose greatest poems – "Aristocrats", "*Vergissmeinnicht*", "How to Kill", and "Enfidaville" – were drafted, if not completed, in the area in the spring of 1943. While Douglas was in camp the place was heavily shelled. The last two verses of "Enfidaville" read:

> Now the daylight coming in from the fields
> like a labourer, tired and sad,
> is peering about among the wreckage, goes
> past some corners as though with averted head
> not looking at the pain this town holds,
> seeing no one move behind the windows.
>
> But already they are coming back: to search
> like ants, poking in the debris, finding in it
> a bed or a piano and carrying it out.
> Who would not love them at this minute?
> I seem again to meet
> the blue eyes of the images in the church.

It was at Enfidaville that the 8th Army's great advance across North Africa came to an end. The town had since been rebuilt in fairly nondescript fashion but west of it is a war cemetery containing the graves of nearly two thousand British and Commonwealth soldiers.

From Enfidaville it is a gentle drive through rolling fields of alfalfa, olive and fruit orchards to Sousse, another port bombed by the Allies in 1943. All was now back in place, the harbour busy with ships loading up the produce of the Sahel and salt from the Halk el Menzel lakes.

All along this coast – Sousse, Monastir, Mahdia, Sfax – successive Roman and Islamic armies have left remnants of their places of worship and their fortresses, their monuments to the dead and their palaces. Sometimes, as in the Great Mosques and *ribats* – fortified monasteries – of Sousse and Monastir, war and worship combine, and it is in the *ribat* of Monastir that Bourguiba has chosen eventually to lie. From the high cliffs above Mahdia you can look down on the port which Phoenicians, Romans and Arabs in turn embellished, and from which in later centuries Barbary pirates and Ottoman Turkish fleets operated.

I based myself at Sousse, setting off one morning early for Kairouan and the next day for El Djem. Nothing I had seen in Iraq prepared me for Kairouan, its ramparts, domes, minarets and towers rising out of the desert like a hallucination. Istanbul has mosques that compare in beauty and situation, but they are integrated into the developing architecture of a city. Kairouan, in contrast, seems to have been dropped, fully fashioned, from heaven, without relation to anything except the desert.

West of Kairouan is Berber country, the desert giving way gradually to forest and rock, and, wedged into the side of a mountain, the village of La Kesra. The inhabitants of La Kesra could be mistaken for monks, for they wear hooded robes even when descending from their citadel to work in the plain. As I watched them go conscientiously about their business it seemed unlikely that they had ever heard there was a war going on in Algeria or, if they had, that they would have cared. Life at La Kesra cannot have changed significantly since the Berbers installed themselves there twelve centuries ago.

You can get to El Djem from Sousse very easily on the comfortable train that shunts its leisurely way south from Tunis to Sousse, Sfax, Gabès and El Marsa, which last is on the Libyan frontier. El Djem is little more than an amphitheatre, but it is one of such huge proportions – scarcely smaller in diameter than the Colosseum in Rome – that it dwarfs everything else for miles around. The syrupy, yellow

163

walls have suffered a series of crude restorations, the most essential of which was required after a tax collector in the eighteenth century obtained permission from the bey of the time to bombard a group of reluctant tax payers who had boarded themselves in.

I made one other excursion while I was in Tunisia, and the purpose of it was simply to reconcile my romantic image of an oasis with the real thing. The reality was not a disappointment.

The lushest oases lie in the southwest of the country, reachable most easily from Gabès, which itself has a coastal oasis set on a headland in the beautiful Gulf of Syrtis. The most accessible of the four major oases – Gafsa, Tozeur, Nefta and Kebili – is Kebili, once a slave market, and still a centre for Berbers and Sudanese blacks. The image that I wanted, and found, was a long, shimmering view of sand dunes and distant mountains, with the brilliant green of a solitary oasis as the only break. Round Kebili the salt desert gives way to sand desert and the oases come like spoor marks, drifts of green in varying sizes hiving off from a central cluster.

At Kebili there are 800,000 palm trees – Tozeur has a mere 250,000 – apparently belonging to semi-nomadic Nefzaoua tribes, who are absent most of the year grazing their camels. The green of the trees was like a blessing, and on the drive back into Gabès I passed scenes of equally vivid colour: Tuareg Bedouins, camel caravans, women in brightly coloured robes bearing water jugs. The desert stretched out swimmingly in every direction, as Delacroix painted it; a smudge of palm tree here, a line of eucalyptus there. The political entanglements of men seemed ephemeral in comparison to nature's art and the artist's capturing of it.

Back in Tunis, negotiations, still about French aerodromes, the presence of the FLN in the country, the alleged involvement of Tunisia in helping refugees to cross the frontier, dragged on. I visited more camps and I listened to more speeches by Bourguiba. Although the war itself had many months to run, Tunisia's part in it soon ceased to be news.

Algerian Refugee Camp, Aïn-Khemouda

You have black eyes,
Four years of age,
A chic, cast-off coat
– pepper-and-salt, double-breasted –
A label naming you "Mohamed",
Some slippers, a squashed felt hat.
Nothing else. And "nothing" means just that.

This camp is your home until – well, until.
A flag flaps on a hill.
The *oued* soon will be dry;
Do you know how to cry?

Smoke curls from the tents
Where women who are not your mother,
Hennaed and trinketed, cook.
Your eyes see but do not look.
And men who are not your father,
Turbaned and burned, sit stiff
In rows, like clay pigeons, on a cliff.
Targets do not easily relax.
Your hair is fair as flax.

Guns rattle the mauve hills
Where the last warmth spills
On villages where once you were
One of a family that died.
Not much else. Just that.

You pull down the brim of your hat.
Who knows what goes on inside?

Tunisian-Algerian Frontier

Two trains converge on single rails,
Machine-guns swivelling on their backs;
Barbed wire twists along the tracks,
Electrified to keep "them" back.
Mines explode when all else fails.

"They" have many faces here,
Who by night attempt the frontier.
Striped hoods reduce the single face
To eyes that just examine space,
Knowing eighty years, or nine.

The mountains do not form a line,
But spread their vertebrae like bones.
The red earth ignites its stones,
Sharp in wastes of alpha grass.
Along the *oued* two camels pass.

End of a War

The time when it all ends
Returning enemies to friends,
Turns also friends to enemies,
Replaces old with new treacheries.

Lovers alone are honest in their lies,
Others must depend on spies,

Emissaries or go-betweens, whose lives
Depend on ambiguities.

Now cortège and ceremonial drums,
White flags fluttering in the blue,
But who any longer believes true
Peace with a cease-fire comes?

Near Carthage

Whiteness so white here it enthralls,
Whiteness of sails and walls,
Sea-salt and soda.

Yet everywhere touched by gold,
Minarets and beaches, the old
Palaces, young skins.

And blue like some lotion
Of heaven on mosque and ocean,
In assassinating eyes.

A conjunction of colours to blind us –
Yet running me through
At every step with reminders
Of hair that was gold, skin white, eyes blue.

African Sentry: Bizerta

A rifle in his hands that might,
At a pinch, fire, if one night
A shadow should surprise him.

It would be reaction to fright.
Yet if, by chance, his aim,
Finding a stray target, should maim,
Panic would follow on delight,
Self-punishment be dire.
Better, all round, that weapons cannot fire,
Like men be issued obsolete.

At the Chabonais

Nothing is all you may
Expect from it, it is certainly
What you will get.
Even the saint's eyes staring
As you watch the baring
Of such soiled and vicarious flesh,
Contain only the jet
Pupils of one who saw to it
His own flaws had a finer mesh.

Rebels in Tunis

Non-existent officially, though persistent
Traffickers in arms, in rumour,
They take the news with great good humour,
At cafés conversant with everyone.
The date palms spatter them with sun.
Yet all the while it's clear
Their closest companion is an idea,
One who has no fear
Of reprisals, nor at the back of his mind
Modifications of any kind.

PART V

London Magazine and Publishing

THE REFUGEE CAMPS haunted me during the summer, as I saw the eyes and features of the four-year-old child, Mohamed, repeated in those of my son. I sent the deliberately simple poems I tried to write about them to Joe Ackerley at the *Listener* and he accepted them, occasionally questioning a word, but otherwise offering no comment.

Later, I began to work on a huge anthology, *The Cricketer's Companion*, which, rather to my surprise, went through several editions and still exists in Penguin. I alternated, as always, between hardly being able to believe my luck in having the job I had and feeling that I ought to be doing something else. Fortunately, I was able to make two days of journalism a week provide the leisure for other, less remunerative kinds of work. I knew what I wanted to do when I was writing about cricket, and I was happy enough most of the time to settle for it. Every so often, all the same, it seemed too time-consuming, its rewards too easily achieved. I had moments of envying those for whom it was their whole life and for whom no other considerations existed. I came to know two sorts of friends, as I had done at Oxford, neither of which had much in common with the other. Since the Jack Squire, village-cricket literary life was exactly what the poetry I most admired was a reaction against, I found myself trying to keep my two lives separate.

In 1961 John Lehmann retired from the editorship of the *London Magazine*, which he had founded in 1954 with the surprising, if brief, support of the *Daily Mirror*. He had, in any case, taken the previous two years off, leaving the editing in the hands of myself and Maurice Cranston. This was not, perhaps, the most successful of John's ventures, largely, I think, because he had grown increasingly reactionary and little that was going on in the arts found much favour with him. His taste, in painting especially, stopped at about 1945. The *London Magazine* never to me looked right, and its contents, for all their individual merit, lacked *New Writing*'s commitment, scope and urgency. The one had belonged to and characterized its time and the other had not.

When John announced that he could no longer keep the magazine going, it seemed to me a decision based on lack of enthusiasm as much as on lack of money. Cecil King had soon withdrawn the *Mirror*'s backing, and other supporters had come and gone, but the magazine had no rivals and there was a place for it. John, however, had always had a touchy and quarrelsome streak, resulting, as in the case of his publishing firm, in the withdrawal of backers at crucial moments.

My father-in-law, Geoffrey Fry, had recently died and it seemed within our resources to take the magazine on rather than let it fold. I knew there would be no future or pleasure in it unless we could make a fresh start, redesigning the cover and the typeface and giving the magazine more visual impact and contemporary flavour. I don't know if John harboured the hope that we might finance the magazine but allow him to continue as editor, but that, I knew, would have been fatal, even if we could have afforded it.

No one likes to give up an enterprise they have themselves started, and I don't suppose John felt any differently from Cyril Connolly fifteen years earlier when the *Observer* had offered to buy *Horizon* in similar circumstances. On that occasion the *Observer*, wanting someone of a younger generation than Cyril, had asked me if I would be willing to take on the editorship of *Horizon* if the deal went through. Assuming that I had been recommended by Cyril, though slightly surprised, I agreed in principle. I was on the best of terms with Cyril, who had made it plain that in his view "a decade of our lives is quite enough to devote to a lost cause such as the pursuit and marketing of quality contemporary writing".

It turned out that he had not been consulted, and when he heard what the *Observer* had in mind got it into his head that I had been scheming behind his back. This was, alas, a typical Connolly reaction, often demonstrated in his relationships with women, as I came to know to my cost. Someone else's interest would miraculously revive in him hitherto dormant passions. The *Observer* had only become interested after Cyril had expressed, in a series of bitter editorials, his disillusion with London's "sterile, traditional literary society which has killed so many finer things than a review of literature and art". The *Observer*'s proposal was to buy the magazine's name and such subscribers as it had and try to give it a new lease of life. In the event Cyril contrived to make the sale of the magazine impossible. For a long time, until evidence was produced to the contrary, he refused to believe that it had not all been my idea.

The *London Magazine*, which in its first incarnation in 1820 had published Hazlitt, Keats, De Quincey and Lamb over nine years, was now faced with the same options: continuing under a different editor or going under. In the end, John seemed relieved to be rid of the worries, though perhaps if I had been a total stranger rather than a wartime protégé it would have made for an easier subsequent relationship. The hand-over went through in amicable fashion, but though I saw John at regular intervals until his death and we remained good friends, he seemed unable to bring himself to make any comment or express any interest in the magazine, which he received free for the next twenty-five years.

As there was going to be no break in production between John Lehmann's magazine and what I was proposing to call *London Magazine: New Series*, I had to start preparing it while John was still technically both proprietor and editor. This was made particularly difficult by John's renewed desire to attend the Charing Cross Road office, something he had scarcely done during the previous two years.

The magazine was being printed by the Shenval Press, as indeed it still is, and I asked James Shand, its unworldly proprietor, to get his typographers Jack Bowles and Ron Costley to produce specimen pages. Jack Bowles spent much of his time on CND activities, so it was Ron who did most of the work, then and subsequently. I wanted to get rid of the cosy, bookish image suggested by the Ardizzone frontispiece used by John, and to replace it with something cleaner and more abstract. I had Ben Nicholson's work in mind. I wanted the New Series to reflect an interest in painting and theatre, as well as in literature. John Whiting, who had recently had a success with his play *The Devils*, had become a friend and he agreed to write regularly for us on the theatre.

I was anxious not to offend John, who was easily enough offended, or to hurt his feelings, but I knew it would be useless if the magazine carried on in his image. Luckily, we shared many friends among contributors and up to a point – the point, I think, at which John had begun to lose sympathy with new developments – many tastes. But I wanted what had previously been a "review of literature" to be more broadly based, more adventurous in what it covered and the way it covered it. As well as reports from correspondents abroad I determined that we would also deal with architecture, cinema and music on a regular basis. All of this we still do.

John at the time had two assistants, Barbara Cooper, dozy, old-maidish and long-established, and Charles Osborne, not long arrived from Brisbane. Unfortunately the magazine's first assistant editor, David Hughes, who had become one of my closest friends, had departed to write novels, work for Rupert Hart-Davis's publishing firm and marry the actress Mai Zetterling.

Charles Osborne, able and good-natured, was keen to stay on, which he did until 1966, when he left to take up what became increasingly stormy duties at the Arts Council. His only failing as far as I was concerned was that whenever my back was turned – and because of my *Observer* work it was turned quite frequently at that time – he would import unspecified Australians into the office to perform nominal duties. Barbara Cooper, much to my relief, decided to leave. Masochistic and fiercely loyal to John, who had mildly ill-treated her for many years, she could contemplate no successor. Overnight, her attitude towards me changed from friendliness to implacable hostility. Self-banished from the centre of things, she contented herself with putting spells on me, which may well have worked.

During those early months John Russell, often in Paris, was invaluable in suggesting, and getting, new contributors. He himself translated Ionesco's *Recollections of Brancusi* for our first issue. Sonia Orwell, or Pitt-Rivers as she was at the time, acted as our French literary scout, until drink and pretentiousness made her too difficult. William Weaver, an American and noted translator from the Italian, became our link with Rome.

That olive-green first number contained poems by Philip Larkin, Derek Walcott and George Barker; a story by Ted Hughes; an article on opera by Bruno Walther; and critical pieces by Harold Acton, John Bayley, Christopher Hollis, John Whiting, George Macbeth and John Fuller. The first in a series of illustrated articles on painting, "Developments in Style", was devoted to Keith Vaughan. The look and feel of the magazine were much as I wanted. The problem now was to find improved distribution and a readership in Connolly's "particularly disheartening centre" as he called London in one of his *Horizon* farewells. In November 1949 Connolly had revealed in another *Horizon* comment that a traveller sent round the cities of northern England had managed to sell only one subscription in a year. Cambridge had never taken more than a dozen copies, and most university towns, except Oxford, less than half that. "In the end," Connolly concluded, "the public gets the magazines it deserves."

I was not unaware of the problems; of the difficulty in getting people to subscribe and the magazine into shops; of dwindling advertising revenue and mounting printing costs. Most of all, how depressing the lack of response could be, an apathy unknown in France and Germany, and hardly prevalent in Italy. In 1961 I set my sights on surviving *Horizon*'s decade. Now, twenty-six years later, though the same problems exist, and in a more extreme form, the magazine means as much to me as it did when that first issue came out.

Contributors to the next few issues included Cyril Connolly, L. P. Hartley, Victor Pasmore, Ben Nicholson, Christopher Isherwood, Bertolt Brecht, Sylvia Plath and Goronwy Rees. I came to realize the necessity of having at least one fairly well-known figure each month, so as to make it possible to introduce new writers and painters without losing the more general reader.

New writers, or those unjustly long out of favour, usually do more for a magazine than those well established. In purely commercial terms this may not be the case, but in the long run a magazine acquires character and freshness of tone from its discoveries, not from the printing of celebrities. I wanted the critical section of the magazine to be as good as I could make it but not to take over. Such magazines as have emerged in the meantime – such as the *London Review of Books* – have been essentially journals of comment; there are even fewer places now for the unknown short-story writer and poet to try their wings.

In 1961 the only other monthly journal of high profile was

Encounter, perennially engaged in the ideological war against communism. Its aims were essentially different from ours: literature and the arts in general were always subservient to foreign affairs and politics. The imbalance has become more pronounced in recent years, though not as marked as it has come to be in the case of the *New Statesman*, whose literary prestige has declined out of all recognition since the days of Kingsley Martin and Raymond Mortimer. As political comment and the coverage of new books in one way or another were not in short supply elsewhere, it seemed much more useful to do something different. The *London Magazine* has rarely published overtly political articles but has treated political issues in literary terms, or as obliquely reflected in poems, travel pieces and stories.

We began life in Charing Cross Road, moving to 30 Thurloe Place three years later, first to two rooms above Martyn Beckett's architect's office and more recently to a studio in the garden of the same building. Thurloe Place is ideal, close to the Underground at South Kensington and therefore handy for contributors and the Shenval messengers, the long line of which began with Fred, a former European flyweight boxing champion, and has included among a variety of colourful characters a sturdy Maori who always wore shorts. I live within walking distance, a bonus equally for me and the office dog.

No one in their right mind would want to run a literary magazine unless it was what they wanted to do more than anything else. For the first ten years of my editorship the *Observer* provided me with an income, and when that came to an end I had to rely on freelance journalism and the writing and editing of books. The magazine always came first and I have never once not looked forward to going into the office, no matter what bills and piles of unsuitable manuscripts might be lurking there. It only needs one good poem or story in the mail, one new subscriber, to make it seem worthwhile.

Knowing the misery of prolonged uncertainty, I resolved from the start not to leave any manuscript unreturned or undecided upon by Friday evening.

Over the years several assistants since Charles Osborne's day – Hugo Williams, Chloe D'Avigdor-Goldsmid, Kate Fleming, Vivien Lewis, Oliver Low, Christopher Hawtree – have done their best with the various business aspects, not a particularly rewarding task, though rarely conducted in gloom. At present the dog is my only member of staff, which means I do the make-up, the pasting up of the galleys and everything else to do with editorial and administrative matters myself. Two libel actions and, after Martyn Beckett's departure, huge increases in rent have produced moments of crisis, and in the hurricane of 18 October 1987 one of the trees that surround us came through the roof. It might have been much worse.

In 1965 we began to publish books, mainly by contributors to the magazine, a natural extension of the magazine itself as I envisaged it. Julian Maclaren-Ross's *Memoirs of the Forties*, Bernard Spencer's *Collected Poems*, Barbara Skelton's *Born Losers*, Gavin Ewart's *Pleasures of the Flesh*, Paul Theroux's *Murder on Mount Holly*, Tony Harrison's *The Loiners*, T. C. Worsley's *Flannelled Fool*, John Whiting's *On Theatre*, Keith Vaughan's *Journals and Drawings* were among our first titles. They have all stood the test of time. Most of our early books were printed by the Shenval Press and they look as good today as when they were published.

From time to time we took on books by writers who had nothing particularly to do with the magazine, but I never wanted to expand to a degree that involved getting in extra staff. Some years we published up to fifteen books; other years as few as three. The last but one of the 150 or so books published between 1965 and 1985 was Jaroslav Seifert's *An Umbrella from Piccadilly*, at that time, 1983, the only book of his poems available in translation. Shortly after it came out he was awarded the Nobel Prize, and after an initial sale of under a hundred copies we had to reprint twice, in editions of a thousand at a time.

There was no point in our taking on books for commercial reasons alone, since we had neither the staff nor the resources, though initially Michael Joseph courteously and efficiently handled our distribution. On the other hand, since the publishing involved virtually no overheads, not even a token salary for myself, the books we did publish had a reasonable chance of breaking even. Most of them did rather better than that. By their nature they were books unlikely to sell widely, but we were able to produce them decently and the writers, if not made exactly rich, probably did at least as well as they expected. We had our libel problems here, too; John Sutro, hitherto a patron of the author, obliged us to withdraw Barbara Skelton's novel *A Love Match*.

As time went by we branched out into more general publishing – two bizarre and extravagantly produced books called *Concrete Poetry* and *Typewriter Art*, occasional books on cricket and racing, books of criticism and children's books, as well as the memoirs, novels and poetry with which we had begun. I thought *Concrete Poetry* would probably bankrupt us, but amazingly it sold out. Overexcited by this, we undertook to do a collection of work by the poet-artist Ian Hamilton Finlay, some of whose most telling images had appeared in *Concrete Poetry*. This mercifully never materialized, for dealings with Finlay, however engaging and maligned a creature he may be in private, tended to end acrimoniously or in protracted legal proceedings. On this occasion the projected book came to an impossible working, a situation that could have been resolved by reducing a poem of some twenty-six pages, each page repeating three or four identical words, something like *Long Horizon Low Fields*, to sixteen pages. Hugo Williams, about to depart to go round the world – we later published his lively account of the journey – diffidently suggested to Finlay that sixteen identical pages could possibly be as effective as twenty-six. The proposal enraged the poet, who made it plain that any publishing house which could entertain so frivolous an idea was certainly not fit to publish him.

Hamilton Finlay's best work, a mixture of visionary ideas, classic design and lyric power, was, despite a certain whimsy, appealing. His well-attested paranoia may have been partly accounted for by ill health and isolation. Twenty years later he got the book he deserved, a handsome volume published under the title *A Visionary Almanac* and devoted to all aspects of this reclusive concrete poet, moralist and gardener. To get the best out of him probably required a visit to his home, Stonypath, in Scotland, where his poems in stone could be seen in their proper setting.

One thing I particularly wanted to do was to experiment with short, high-quality books in paperback – novellas, essays, memoirs, poems – that, despite short runs, could be produced and sold cheaply. Accordingly, I asked Ron Costley at Shenval to look out for various kinds of coarse paper, the consistency of packing material, to use as covers. I knew exactly what I wanted, something serviceable and rough, yet distinctive and appetizing. "All these *London Magazine* Editions", *The Times* described the first batch, "have a tough format with large black type, stitched spines, and a sensible healthy look like wholemeal sandwiches cut narrow for the traveller's pocket." In the *New Statesman* they were described as "cheap and elegant". The *Sunday Telegraph* remarked that the series offered "minority writing of exceptional quality". This was a pleasing response, and in all we produced some twenty volumes between 1966 and 1968, most of them costing 6s.6d. – approximately 30p. They varied in length from 60 pages to 200 pages, and we printed either 1000 or 2000 copies.

The first batch of four consisted of Robert Rushmore's novella *A Passion for Meddling*, Robin Fulton's translations of four contemporary Italian poets, John Whiting's theatre articles, and a series called *Leaving School*, in which writers described their first steps into the adult world and which we had run in the magazine. We followed this up with Brian Jones's poems, Gordon Meyer's short stories, a book of shell drawings by Philip Sutton and a biography of Sidney Keyes. Heere Heeresma's short novel *A Day at the Beach* came next, the subject in due course of a film by Roman Polanski, followed by a bilingual anthology of contemporary Italian verse.

It was an interesting venture while it lasted, but the cost of producing the books began to escalate alarmingly, so that although their scope and nature did not change their cover price would have had to increase. Unfortunately, too, the majority of booksellers did not really take to them, commenting that they looked lost on their shelves. Had we had the resources to provide special holders and to embark on a real marketing campaign the outcome might have been different. As it was, Geoffrey Holloway's *Rhine Jump* became a Poetry Book Society choice, Brian Jones's poems were reprinted twice, and a book we did on Greek shadow puppets sold out. I am always coming across people who collected the books and remember them with affection, as I still do.

When I look at the shelves that contain the fruits of those twenty years of publishing, 1966–86, I feel a proprietary pride; not because they were all successful, but because I really wanted to do each one. Perhaps most publishers feel this, but when there are no commercial pressures on you to publish anything at all – no staff to occupy, no machines to keep turning – every book taken on represents a purely gratuitous act. Publishing has always been for me an amateur activity in the strictest sense of the word; it was never my livelihood, nor have I ever earned a penny out of it. But, since it was a labour of love, there was all the more reason for it to be done to the highest professional standards. A small firm, which cannot justify having its own sales force and has to attach itself to a larger organization, can never expect to achieve quite the same impact as if the reps were working for that house alone. The advantages are that you have total control over the design of the book – its typeface, binding and jacket – as well as over the print run. When there are only two people involved – the author and yourself – it becomes the friendliest of collaborations.

There was only one significant exception to this and that was when Costas Taktsis, a Greek novelist of great distinction but deeply masochistic habits, complained about the translation of his book. It was, on the best of independent authorities, a brilliant version, but the author, whose own English, to say the least, was imperfect insisted on querying every sentence. He became tearful, hysterical and abusive, refusing to leave the office unless the translator – an Englishman working in Athens and married to a Greek – was replaced. I cajoled and pleaded with him but he refused to budge. No, Costas said, he wanted someone else, his masterpiece was being ruined. How could he tell, I asked, when his own English was so poor and two bilingual Greeks whom I had consulted both thought the translation as near to flawless as any translation could be? He could feel it, he said, eyes rolling and tubby body quivering with rage. Well, we can't stay here all night – it was by now eight o'clock – I said, picking up my keys, we'll have to discuss it tomorrow. I'm not going – Costas stamped his foot – you can lock me in.

It was only when I threatened to have him hosed out by the Fire Brigade or to hurl him downstairs that he began to bridle accommodatingly. Eventually, hustled down four flights of stairs feet scarcely touching the ground, he ended up on his bottom and beaming. Next day he was back for more, but this time we settled on going through together every sentence in his 300-page novel, a task that took several days but which seemed like months. In the end Costas, for all his disputatiousness, could find scarcely half a dozen phrases worth altering.

He was an unhappy man, greatly gifted, most at ease in women's clothes, a taste not unusual among Greek artists of the period.

Besides Taktsis, our foreign authors included his fellow Greek Andreas Embiricos, the strangest novelist on our list and the author of an unpublished erotic masterpiece *The Great Eastern*, Marc Peyre, whose novel had a preface by Lawrence Durrell and was translated by Durrell's wife, the Sicilian Elio Vittorini, the Italians Eugenio Montale and Renzo Rosso, the banned Czechoslovak Ludvik Vaculik, the Indian novelist Nayantara Sahgal, niece of Pandit Nehru, the Americans Charles Bukowski, Louis Simpson, Paul Theroux, Jeffrey Meyers, Seymour Krim and Dotson Rader. We published the poems of the Germans Reiner Kunze and Rose Ausländer, the Swedes Tomas Tranströmer and Gunnar Harding, and a Finnish anthology edited for us by Herbert Lomas.

Barbara Skelton, no longer Mrs Connolly, was the first English novelist we published and Graham Swift was the most recent. In between there were the first novels of Ursula Holden, Patrice Chaplin, John Ginger and Michael Feld, two novels by J. L. Carr and a book of short stories by the West Indian Clyde Hossein.

Publishing Roy Fuller's three volumes of memoirs, as well as poems by him, gave me as much pleasure as anything. He had been a friend from the very beginning, a writer who moved effortlessly from poetry to prose and back again, never producing anything that did not have its own unmistakable watermark. Julian Symons, almost as old a friend, had contributed various semi-autobiographical pieces to the magazine and these we published under the title *Notes from Another Country*. John Mellors, later to become the magazine's main novel reviewer, produced two books of memoirs, about his Army days in India and his time as an advertising executive, that were sad, funny and altogether delightful. Maclaren-Ross's *Memoirs of the Forties* and T. C. Worsley's *Flannelled Fool* were the sort of hybrid books

I liked doing and they probably attracted as much attention as anything we ever did.

It was, of course, a luxury to be able to publish as much or as little as we liked, the only real anxiety being that if successive books failed to pay their way then the day of reckoning would come sooner rather than later. In fact, there was no such moment; rather a feeling that it was time I should try and write my own books. The magazine was enough of a tie and a responsibility. I was always pleased, rather than annoyed, when critics who had been brought up on the magazine – Frank Marcus, our theatre critic and author of *The Killing of Sister George*, Stephen Gardiner, who wrote regularly on architecture for us, and William Feaver, for example – were taken up by national newspapers, and I was equally glad when writers whose first books we had published moved on to larger publishers who could do more for them. That was part of the point. There is more to be gained by helping writers on the way up – or on the way down for that matter – when you are acting on our kind of scale, than by taking the safer course.

Portoferraio

The afternoon like dead skin; now heat bores
Relentlessly through shutters; you turn, half-pause
In combing salt out from your hair.
Outside, steps hesitate, continue on stone stair.
Beneath us, boats seem stuck over glass; walls
The colour of pollen crumble by water; a child calls.
The harbour looks oiled and heavy; lines of palms,
Dusty and grey, raise supplicating arms.
I watch you move against the mirror, beyond
The silver of your hairbrush see flies stalk

Across the bedspread; and when you talk
Our eyes meet in the glass, in the glass grow fond.

Antwerp: Musée des Beaux Arts

Rubens, De Vos, Memling – room after room
Of imperious and crusted flesh, luxuriantly
Spread under cavaliers and Christs, under eyes
Of students scrutinizing the texture of tombs.
The oyster light and dedicated thought
Create their own life, placidly sensuous,
Away from the glitter and moan of the port.

Outside, in wafer-thin air, women hurry by,
Flesh no longer proud, and shapeless with suffering,
Or boredom, or both. Banana boats
Hoot over cobbled streets, inscribe in pale sky
Their steamy messages. But only hidden under
Paint, centuries-down in these cavernous rooms,
Do the senses, passionate as thunder,
Stretch themselves out, and like boats passing the boom
At sunset, reach open sea, a spiritual south.

For a London Child

Sleep where the plane tree nets you with shadow,
A geranium like a lamp at your elbow.

Sleep to the rocking rhythm of trains,
The scent of petunias blooded by June rains.

Sleep by a sea of asphalt, rubbery with heat,
People's voices stones thrown from the street.

Sleep in dreams whose glances are all loving,
Now when the clock is steady, before the hands start moving.

Sleep to the query of dogs, muzzles glinting like metal,
Whose own mouth knows only the breast's white milkfall.

Sleep now, wool mariner, on waves of content,
Admiral of innocence, scrutinizing and silent.

Sleep where green leaves feather the stone
Urns stained by winter, falling for you alone;

Who wait your first winter, child still cocooned
From cold, a half-sketched poem, mandolin not yet tuned.

Sleep in your image of sailor or poet, explorer, engine driver,
Child of two kisses, on your brow a four-leaved clover.

Koala

How should I describe you – eternal
Image of the cuddly bear, solace
Of your button-nosed familiars of every race,
Who on cold nights or those long cheerless
Afternoons, when to be small
Is to be misunderstood, clasp your toy belly and kiss
Injustice away – whom to possess most surely is to miss.

Drawing your iron-bark claws along my wrist
You narrow two rheumy eyes where indifference
Has laid a deposit of pink mist –
Your hold on life so delicate,
That to lessen those twin and absorbing opiates
You live on – ladles of sleep and of eucalypt,
Storehouses of bored over-intelligence

Into which you continually dip – would be to remove
For ever the Empire's one pure Existentialist.
Fatalist, addict, catalyst
Of early but enduring emotions, you lay like a glove
A clenched fist over mine, twitching a tar
Nose as if it was snuff not gum leaves you sniff –
Crybaby, as passive as a teddy, you simply *are*.

And restoring you to that high fork
In the tree where the juiciest morsels bunch,
I watch you pluck with the tiniest tremble a stalk,
Thrusting the gum sap home with a crunch
Like the breaking of celery, passenger to oblivion –
Perfervid muncher, whom tomorrow I shall come upon
Sun-doped and happy, a gnawed twig in your paw like a pen.

Zoo

The smell assaults you first, from places
Where nightly the padded steps rehearse
Africa's movements in its restless sleep.
Here all our captive faults are nursed
Brooding in their sultry paces.

Like phrases they turn and reiterate
Lost meanings in their striped and alien cages,
Pausing to blink a heavy eye at sun
That curls the pallid ends of pages
In their history blanked out and done.

Now nothing in their world remains
Where always on a straw-laid floor
They meditate, like prisoners in a war
Fought for lost causes, whose mere act
Of living forced them to participate.

187

Ignorant of ends and means, knowing
Only the blank reality of exile, they seek
The one vivid proof of life, their shadow,
That alone answers when they speak –
A familiar whom, a little way behind, they tow.

Watching, we turn our backs and move away,
Suddenly ashamed and moved by some glint
Of pity in their shooting eyes, as if today
They showed some symptom or some hint
Of our predicament tomorrow, or the next day.

PART VI

Sussex Connections

SHORTLY BEFORE I left for Australia to cover the 1954/5 MCC
tour and soon after our son Jonathan was born, we found a
house in Sussex that fulfilled all requirements – mine at any
rate: downland country, a smell of the sea and a situation
within easy reach of Hove cricket ground. The village of
Clayton, immediately below the two landmark windmills of
Jack and Jill (one of them inhabited by the golf journalist and
commentator Henry Longhurst) clusters round a narrow lane
that twists and turns along the northern slope of the Downs.
Our house, which in its day had been successively Roman
villa, farm and, more recently, rectory, looked westwards
through an orchard, past Clayton church and farm, towards
the great hump of Wolstonebury, whose slopes were rusted
with beech woods. Sheer to the south the sky was bisected by
the line of the Downs, crowding in and falling away as far as
the eye could see. The front of the house, itself on a slope, was
grey stucco with bow windows, the back red brick. A small
courtyard, its overlooking windows shuttered in the French
style, separated the house from the lane. The grounds consisted
of several fields, lawns front and back, a pond and a circular
walled garden adjoining a converted stable. In due course we
added streams and a water garden. The property had been
left empty for some time and after its multiple wartime

occupation was in bad shape. We bought it for £6000.

Although Clayton was secluded, Hove cricket ground was only a twenty-minute drive away. Hassocks station, from where you could get to Victoria in fifty minutes, was a mile and a half distant. Lewes was seven miles; Plumpton race-course three. From my arrival from India in 1932 until I departed into the Navy ten years later, Sussex had been the nearest thing to home. My parents, on their various leaves from Calcutta, rented houses for the summer at Halland and Eastbourne, but mostly my base had been Ardingly Rectory, a "holiday home" for boys with parents abroad. During the holidays from school at Forest Row, and later from Haileybury, we bicycled all over mid Sussex, in search mainly of cricket grounds and cinemas.

During my sea-time I use to dream of Sussex; not so much a specific Sussex as a generalized, romantic image conjured out of memory and hope. Sussex cricket played a large part in it, to the extent that I had only to see the word Sussex written down, in whatever context, for a shiver to run down my spine. Such an association might only properly belong to adolescence, but it has survived. Now the dream was a reality and for the next twenty-five years Sussex was my home, London a mere work-place.

As well as its other strategic advantages, proximity to Brighton among the most important, Clayton was within easy reach of several close friends. Cyril Connolly, now married to Deirdre Craven, with whom I had once been involved, was initially installed at one of Lord Gage's farm lodges near Firle, then at Eastbourne; William Plomer had moved from Rustington in West Sussex to an even more nondescript bungalow in Hassocks; Cuthbert Worsley, after a spell in our converted stable following a disastrous attempt to live on a boat, ended up in Brighton. Brighton also housed at various times Francis King, Frank Tuohy, John Haylock and Robin Maugham. If Bernard Gutteridge was marooned, carless, in Graffham

192

Act of Darkness

further to the west, Derek Verschoyle, his neighbour at Lurga-shall, suffered no such restrictions.

Cyril's move to Eastbourne, necessitated by Lord Gage's wanting his house for one of his managers, was perhaps the most surprising, but it seemed to suit him. He trundled up to London once a week to the *Sunday Times*; otherwise he seemed moderately content to potter conjugally about the shops in Lewes or Eastbourne. Every fortnight or so we met *en famille* – the Connollys by now having acquired a daughter, and some years later a son – either at Clayton or their house.

Occasionally Cyril and I would lunch halfway, at the White Hart in Lewes, all *froideurs* over women and misunderstandings about *Horizon* finally resolved. He was avid for, and eager to provide, gossip, though at times his successive obsessions with missing diplomats, the murder of Lord Errol and the Lord Lucan affair obliterated even his anxieties for hard news about the romantic and sexual activities of his friends, the misfortunes of his imagined and real enemies.

The *Sunday Times* connection, without which Cyril's extrava-gance would have been crippled, absolved him in his own eyes from more imaginatively demanding work. What annoyed him most was when well-meaning acquaintances, fellow guests at a dinner party perhaps, asked him what he was writing, as if his Sunday articles had been done in his sleep. In fact, by the time he had read the book, written his piece, taken it up to London, at the same time acquiring another book or books to review, there was not all that much of his week left. He no longer, in any case, showed signs of further literary ambition, preferring to collect reviews and travel pieces in volumes ran-domly put together, their occasional nature disguised by cun-ning introductions.

By the time he had moved to Eastbourne his book collection, preserved behind glass-fronted cases, absorbed most of his attention. He handled books as he did choice fruit, greedily but appreciatively. He loved them for what they were physically, for what they contained and for their associations. Their market value was also not without interest, for he was usually hard up, and tactical sales, of manuscripts as well as books, had frequently to be made.

Cyril, the most transparent liar and least successful dissembler of guilt of anyone I have known, had the rare gift of being able to involve you in his own interests and intrigues while at the same time becoming obsessive about yours. He himself needed intrigues as fish need water, as a confirmation of his social existence. He was, unlike John Lehmann, always interested in what was in the *London Magazine* and helpful with suggestions. Although his interest in any form of sport was minimal he used to touch me by reading my reports and making reference to cricketers of the day, smiling proudly, like a small boy, at his prowess. "Tom Graveney must have hooked well yesterday," he would say, having mugged it up, and delighted at the incongruity of his own words.

Cyril's flaws of character, described with both relish and affection by Barbara Skelton in her diaries *Tears before Bedtime*, were too obvious to need emphasizing but for anyone who became his friend and shared his interests he was the best companion imaginable. There was nothing that could not be discussed, and such was his sensibility that confidences exchanged with him were as if with a woman. Jealous to a degree, he could snap like a crocodile, but in later years there was little reason. Barbara appears to have immortalized his "Chinese coolie legs" but conventionally plain though he may have been, when his eyes lit up or he laughed he had irresistible charm, gaiety mingled with boyish mischievousness.

On the telephone Cyril cultivated a conspiratorial purr, a slightly effete throatiness. For him the telephone was largely an instrument for the surreptitious transmitting and receiving of classified information. Had he not been so hopeless a deceiver, he would have flourished as a spy, because planned subterfuge took the place of exercise in his scheme of things.

He had, however, one disconcerting telephone habit, of some psychological interest. Whereas there are those who cannot relinquish a conversation without endlessly repeating the same phrases anticipatory to ringing off, Cyril went to the other extreme, simply putting the phone down without any farewells at all. Whoever he was talking to would be left in mid air, and at some disadvantage.

By the time Cyril came to Sussex the animals in his life had been replaced by children. They were more portable and less damaging. He had become obliged, after some years of resenting the idea, to accept himself as a family man, a creature more inhibited in range of activity and in movement than he would have liked, but one who, by his lights, tried to do his duty. Sex, too, he appeared to regard in a sunset light. "It's not the ability that goes," he confided to me one evening, without evident regret, "it's the desire."

In trying to find a title for his last book of essays – eventually *The Evening Colonnade* was settled on – Cyril confessed that though he *was* a critic "on the bias, on the hop, on the run, on the slide, in the sun, in the shade, in the galleys", he didn't want to be called a critic. Questioned by an interviewer about whether he saw the rest of his life in terms of his library and of reflections on the past, or whether there were other things he wanted to do, he replied, "I should like to see a great many more elephants in the wild. I have a deep devotion to them, I can't have enough. I agree with Donne: 'Nature's great master-peace: an Elephant, The only harmlesse great thing . . .'."

From time to time Cyril did get to see an elephant or two, though mostly, during the last decade of his life, the weekly stint tethered him. But what might have seemed hack-work in other hands rarely seemed so in his: everything he wrote, whether on other writers, architects, politicians, food, art, psychiatry, gardens – as governed by the books he was required to review – emerged wonderfully fresh, concise

195

and imaginatively rehoused. I never thought very highly of his taste in pictures or his judgement of contemporary poets, but placing was never one of his virtues as a critic. He wrote a prose that was more allusive, suggestive and elegant than perhaps anyone else of his time; a prose at once reflective, wise and just. It may have been the prose of a man who was vulnerable, greedy, devious and susceptible to most vices, but in the last resort, perhaps because of all this and despite his own frequent depressions and disappointments, it was able miraculously to convey the excitement of reading and travelling, loving and looking, study and nature. His gloom was often infectious, but his high spirits were equally so. He could be rude, cruel and vindictive, but he was never pompous, self-important or affected. I remember his saying once, in relation to John Betjeman's popularity as a performer and general social equanimity, "Well, of course, John used to have to sing for his supper." It would not have been unfair to have pointed out that, in terms of reliance on patronage and social favour, so too did Cyril, though the song a well-meaning hostess sometimes got was not what she had bargained for.

When he began eventually to go downhill – a cataract operation being succeeded by the illness that killed him – he could scarcely eat or drink anything, though he continued to take meticulous care over the wine and food for his guests. Shortly before he died I spoke to him in hospital. To my question about how he felt he replied, "Liver's lousy." Instead of his putting the receiver down I heard it drop from his hand and lie on the bed, the sounds of the room like the sea in a shell continuing to reverberate. They were the last words I heard him say.

Cyril wrote two longish pieces for the magazine, one called "The Breakthrough in Modern Verse", the other on art nouveau, as well as a parody of Ian Fleming, "Bond Strikes Camp", which we eventually published separately. Cyril probably spent too much energy on parodies, though those of his youth have dated less than most. Ian, with whom I stayed several years running in Jamaica, was briefly also a Sussex friend, though he lived in Kent. The circumstances were sad, for after his second and most severe heart attack he was banished to the Dudley Hotel in Hove. It was hoped he would have peace and quiet there, and, especially, be at a safe distance from his wife, whose presence towards the end accounted for a dangerous rise in his pulse rate. Ann remained constitutionally unable to avoid irritating Ian or to adjust her noisy social life to accommodate his.

During the weeks Ian was at Hove we would lunch at the Dudley and if Sussex were playing at the county ground drive there for the afternoon. Ian's idea of giving up smoking on doctor's orders was to cut down from sixty a day to thirty, smoked as usual from a holder, and on instruction he reduced his intake of Vodka Martini from three lethal doses to one. He was very shaky, his normally brick-red complexion the dry mauve of a paper flower. On our last visit to the county ground before he was foolishly adjudged fit to return to Sandwich and further exacerbation, we saw Ted Dexter make a brilliant hundred, something Ian had been keen to see at least once. Within a fortnight he was dead.

It was Ian's custom to name minor characters in his novels after his friends. Commander Ross, a secret agent in whose image I received a welcome promotion, appears in *The Man with the Golden Gun*, a book for which I gave Ian only too familiar details about ECT, a treatment Bond is obliged to undergo. Unfortunately, the Commander does not play a large part in the plot, a KGB agent called "Pistols" Scaramanga murdering him and disposing of his body in a pitch lake in Trinidad.

Ian was a creature of unvarying habit. In London I never saw him when he was not wearing a dark blue suit, spotted bow tie, and blue shirt. In a restaurant he never ordered anything other than triple scrambled egg and smoked salmon.

No doubt he wore other clothes and ate other food in restaurants but I never witnessed it. He had the largest handwriting of anyone who ever wrote to me, the letters angular and slanting, and of a size suitable for the almost blind. Not many of his wife's friends cared for him, a feeling that was reciprocated, but to me he was a good and entertaining friend and I missed him greatly.

Cuthbert Worsley, until the arrival of William Plomer in Hassocks, became our nearest neighbour. He wrote only once for the magazine, a spirited defence of his friend Terence Rattigan at the time of Rattigan's total eclipse, which was due partly to the scorn of Kenneth Tynan. Shortly after our publishing firm had come into existence, however, we received the manuscript of *Flannelled Fool*, a fragment of autobiography about Worsley's childhood, his period of teaching at Wellington and brief Air Force career. I read it at a sitting and cabled acceptance to Worsley, who happened to be in Monte Carlo losing what little money he had at the casino.

I knew Cuthbert only slightly, having written some reviews for him when he was literary editor of the *New Statesman*. He had published a number of my poems during his time there and I had found him a helpful though exacting taskmaster. He still had the manner and appearance of a schoolmaster, though rather a giggly one. In the early days of our acquaintanceship he used to make me feel politically frivolous, but by the time he settled in Sussex his views were as reactionary as they had earlier been left-wing.

We received *Flannelled Fool* shortly after Maclaren-Ross's *Memoirs of the Forties* had come out; perhaps because of it. At least three leading publishers had turned it down on legal advice and Cuthbert himself admitted he had been warned that it was folly to expect publication. Rereading it now I feel there were good reasons for anxiety, but at the time, with little to lose and admiring the book so much, it seemed to me worth the risk. I have in any case a weakness for school stories. Worsley had assured me that all the "college" masters likely to cause trouble were dead, and Kurt Hahn, for whom Cuthbert had briefly taught at Gordonstoun and whose potential reaction had done most to scare off the other publishers, was safely, we hoped, back in Germany. There remained an air commodore, whose whereabouts were unknown, and one or two others who could conceivably kick up a fuss.

In the event nothing happened. Far from closing the firm down before we had hardly started and putting Cuthbert and me in jail, the book got a wonderful press, sold well and reprinted. It is now, twenty years later, a Hogarth Press paperback.

The success of *Flannelled Fool* melted the resistance that the traumatic events described in the book – events of thirty to forty years earlier – had built up in Worsley; this despite many costly and in his opinion wasted years of analysis. Since the prewar publication of *Behind the Battle*, an account of his adventures in Spain as the driver of a blood-transfusion unit during the Civil War, and in 1940 *Barbarians and Philistines*, an educational pamphlet subtitled "Democracy and the Public Schools", he had written no further books in the intervening twenty-five years. The impulse that had produced poems and sketches during the early schoolmastering days appeared to have frozen for good. The release effected by the publication of *Flannelled Fool* – from guilt, among other things, about the childhood drowning in his presence of a loved younger brother – only lasted for five years, but those years were the most productive of Worsley's life.

Flannelled Fool is in part about education, the arbitrary nature of a career and coming to terms with homosexuality. I tried to dissuade Worsley from using the description "This is the self-portrait of a case of arrested development" which he asked me to put on the original blurb, but he insisted, and of course in a way it was true. I jibbed at it, perhaps, because although our backgrounds and sexual tastes were different, we shared the same passion for games, this addiction in both instances outlasting school and university. In my own case I was not inclined to regard this as inhibiting or even limiting, especially since it had paid for a long period of my life. In Worsley's case "innocence", as he described it – he confessed that up until the age of nineteen he knew nothing about masturbation, an extraordinary feat for one who had been to a public school – lasted too long, so that coupled with his sexual immaturity it brought him, once his eyes were opened to the apparently real world, to look back on his days of athletic glory as largely spurious. It was predictable of him that, once initiated into political thinking and writing, the puritanical side of him would dominate his judgements. In this respect he was like a reformed rake, a transformation that eventually took another turn. At the same time he retained his pleasure and interest in sport to the end of his life, as well as gambling recklessly on horses and in casinos.

Everything that happened to Worsley between leaving Marlborough and joining the staff of the *New Statesman* in 1939 can be found in his book. At Marlborough he was in the cricket XI for three years as an opening batsman and wicketkeeper. He played once, as he mentions, for Cambridge. It was an unnerving experience, since the usual wicketkeeper had been injured and Cuthbert was called in at the last moment, never having previously kept wicket to any of the university bowlers.

The match was against Yorkshire at Fenners, and the Cambridge opening bowler bowled huge inswingers of a kind Cuthbert had never seen. Four times in succession in the first over they pitched around middle stump and, hidden from view by a burly pair of Yorkshire buttocks, disappeared down to the long leg boundary. At the end of the over the Yorkshire total was 16, batsman No. 1, 0; batsman number 2, 0; extras 16. At this point the drizzle that had been threatening turned into a deluge and play was abandoned for the day. In fact there was no more play in the match, so for the best part of three days Cuthbert had to endure the humiliating sight of an unchanged scoreboard, witness to a record of its kind.

By the time the war finished Cuthbert had settled in at the *New Statesman* and exchanged an unsatisfactory heterosexual marriage for the first of two or three homosexual versions. At the *New Statesman* he succeeded V. S. Pritchett as literary editor, eventually becoming the paper's theatre critic. As a result he tended to move in theatrical rather than literary circles. The emphysema, a consequence of his compulsive smoking, that for many years had plagued him, as it did Ken Tynan, obliged him to give up the theatre in 1964. Instead, he wrote a weekly article on television for the *Financial Times*, the first critic to deal with the subject on anything other than a superficial level. He did this for nine years, a period during which he produced *Flannelled Fool*, *Fellow Travellers*, a fictionalized memoir of the Spanish War, a short theatrical novel called *Five Minutes, Sir Matthew* and *The Ephemeral Art*, a selection of his television pieces. We published all of these, with modest success. Cuthbert wanted more than anything during these years to have a play performed, but though he finished a couple he had no luck.

By 1971 Cuthbert's emphysema had become so bad that he could only walk short distances without having to bend over, his hands on his knees, to get his breath back. It used to madden him when, coming back from the theatre on the last train, he had to resort to this passive leapfrog position on the long Brighton platform, only for some fellow passenger to come up and ask semi-solicitously whether he was all right. "Had a spot too much to drink, old man?"

Overnight, or so it seemed, Cuthbert took it into his head that he would be better off living in the south and on a boat. He sold his flat, sinking all his capital in an ancient trawler, the idea being that he would sail it through the canals of France and fetch up in some quiet Mediterranean harbour, preferably near a casino. As usually happens, the boat he bought needed more repairs than he had bargained for and they took a long time. He and John Luscombe, with whom he had lived for several years, stayed meanwhile in our converted stable, with a view of the Downs from every room.

By the time the boat was pronounced seaworthy and suitably equipped winter had arrived. Instead of sailing leisurely south in warm weather they set off in an autumn gale. The boat developed one defect after another, the heating packed up, and in an appalling winter the French canals froze over. Stranded at Arles they had eventually to abandon the whole idea, leaving the boat to be sailed back by a hired crew. It was later sold at a crippling loss.

When Cuthbert arrived back in England he was in a bad way. Even if things had turned out differently, life on board, with its draughts and damp, its endless bending and climbing, would have been fatal for him. He and Johnny returned to Clayton, moving later to a house in Rottingdean rented from Enid Bagnold and settling ultimately in a flat overlooking the sea at Brighton. For a few years, despite lack of money and increasing immobility, things seemed bearable. They came over most weeks for Sunday lunch, Cuthbert stick-thin and eating little. On 23 February 1977, finding the effort no longer worthwhile, Cuthbert went to bed, taking a bottle of whisky with him. He drank some of the whisky and with it swallowed a bottleful of sleeping tablets, a quantity that the Coroner, with a curious urge to precision, described as the largest overdose he had ever encountered.

Johnny Luscombe reverted to being a butler, a job he had done before but had no real need to do again. Gentle except when drunk, self-effacing, and an intelligent, sweet-natured companion, he had had much to cope with as Cuthbert's health declined. Twenty years younger than Cuthbert, he was a pick-up that turned out well. He frequently and not surprisingly fretted at the restricting circumstances of their relationship, yet when Cuthbert's death left him free, and with enough money, he found himself without resources and without desire. Nothing we suggested to him took his fancy. Then one day he was gone, having successfully answered an advertisement for staff from a septuagenarian bachelor of the Oppenheimer family who bred bull terriers on a large estate near the Thames. Weeks later he wrote, saying he was back in uniform, second butler, and in his disguise occasionally serving guests with whom he and Cuthbert had once been friends. He came to lunch on his day off from time to time, but despite some comical stories he was not the same. The butler's uniform had remoulded him and he had gone back in time, reduced in spirit and ambition. After an unusually long silence a letter arrived from his sister saying that he, too, had taken an overdose.

Though Cuthbert and Johnny were both extraordinarily boyish in appearance, the difference in age made them seem like master and pupil. Cuthbert, bespectacled, lanky, with short back and sides, the ends often sticking out in spikes, never lost a slightly schoolmasterly manner; Johnny was sallow, neatly presentable, deferential.

In his teaching days Cuthbert had been a man with a mission. *Flannelled Fool* is initially about a battle: the struggle for power between the entrenched old guard and a handful of rebels among the staff of an ultraconservative, military-orientated public school. Anyone who was at Wellington during those years, such as Gavin Ewart, will confirm that Cuthbert brought a breath of life to the teaching and general atmosphere of the school. There can be no doubt but that he was an inspiring teacher, able to convey to all but the laziest of boneheads some of the excitement he himself had only recently begun to discover in contemporary literature. Every school needs such a master, a natural ally to the more intelligent boys, to whom he is nearer in age and outlook than he is to most of his colleagues, and Worsley was such a master for Wellington. He had all the attributes for being an immense influence for the good, except perhaps tact and patience. In the end his growing desire to prove himself as a writer made the prospect of becoming a housemaster, with increasing responsibilities, appear insupportable. He was almost certainly sensible to give up when he did, despite the fact that "the great wide world" of his imagination turned out to be less welcoming than he expected.

As the years went by Cuthbert modified many of his views, probably more even than most of his generation. In conversation he was sharp, perceptive, funny. He and Cyril had a healthy respect for each other, but a certain wariness rather than a feeling of friendship was communicated when they were together, as they often were at Clayton.

I have a photograph of Cuthbert, taken in the garden on a very hot summer day when Roy and Kate Fuller, and Julian and Kathleen Symons had driven down from Blackheath. Cuthbert is wearing a broad-brimmed straw hat of vaguely Mexican provenance tilted forward over his nose, his pose one of quizzical attention. Enthusiasm and slight mockery were woven together in his character, the pupil and the schoolmaster sharing the same face. He was the least camp and affected of men, with a contempt for the pretentious and the shallow, the fashionable and the tendentious. It was typical of him that at the time of Terence Rattigan's greatest unpopularity he should come to his defence, not just because he was a friend, but because the ideas and values Rattigan represented in his plays, though temporarily derided, and the skilful, craftsmanlike way he dealt with them, were to Cuthbert the very stuff of drama. In Rattigan's plays miscarriages of justice, misapprehensions about character, tests of loyalty are common themes. Rattigan himself lived the grand life, with houses in Belgravia and Bermuda, and a white Rolls-Royce, in which he used to appear at Clayton. Cuthbert was not immune to grandeur and no less glad of an occasional crumb than was Cyril in similar circumstances, but he was not deceived by trappings. Rattigan wrote compassionately about men who wished to present a face to the world that was at variance with the truth they knew about themselves. Cuthbert understood such a necessity and valued the compassion.

One September, when we had rented a villa in Forio d'Ischia belonging to William Walton, Terry Rattigan had appeared next door, having taken the main house. Ischia in those days, though relatively quiet and, compared to Capri, unfashionable, had such regular summer visitors as Alberto Moravia, Wystan Auden and Lawrence Durrell. The daily arrival on the beach of the Rattigan entourage, famous actors, agents, directors and camp followers, the latter attending with hampers and iced Martinis, was an event. Cuthbert, whom I then scarcely knew, was of the party but in appearance stuck out like a sore thumb among such modish figures. Rattigan only wanted to talk about cricket, though he intrigued me once by stating that a manuscript page of dialogue occupied two minutes on stage, a whole play requiring only sixty pages. I realized that they had more in common than seemed likely, the *New Statesman* critic and Spanish War veteran on the one hand, and the celebrated playwright, now out of fashion, on the other. Three years had separated the appearance of Worsley for Marlborough against Rugby at Lord's and that of Rattigan for Harrow – in the same team as Victor Rothschild – against Eton. Both were opening batsmen. It was an unexpected bond, though they had much else in common: romantic vulnerability, generosity, compulsive gambling. The milky-blue waters of the Gulf of Naples, on this occasion, appeared to have less attraction for either of them than the green of casinos, golf-courses, racecourses and cricket pitches.

In that Sussex triangle formed by Hassocks, Brighton and Eastbourne the person whose life overlapped most with our own was William Plomer. I had first met William when I was a Sub-Lieutenant and he was working alongside Ian Fleming in Naval Intelligence. He was often to be seen at John Lehmann's parties, where the talk flowed more easily than the drink: a tall, urbane, bespectacled figure, with the manner and dress of a senior civil servant or diplomat. He had, in speech, an extra degree of courtesy, the kind of formal refinement one associates with a mandarin. Charles Causley aptly described his voice as having a faintly ecclesiastical boom, "the voice, perhaps, of a mischievous archdeacon with a sideline in African magic".

There was certainly something mischievous about William, about his eyes and mouth especially, that belied the conventional man of letters and publisher. He dressed a part, rather as Eliot did, but while Eliot carried the impersonation through, William always suggested a charade.

He loved storms and tales of disaster, particularly if there was an element of the absurd and grotesque about them. No one was allowed to know more than an allotted aspect of him; the surface was so entertaining, the solicitousness so beguiling, that the occasion for penetrating further never arose. He was at once retiring and sociable; unworldly enough to settle for matchbox life in Adastra Avenue, Hassocks, a singularly undistinguished housing estate on which his own bungalow was the plainest of them all, and yet gregarious enough to be on endless committees and a regular at literary parties, to be on intimate terms with the Queen Mother and various duchesses, a confidant of Forster and Britten and a kindly adviser of the young. What was more, away from Hassocks, he was a performer: an accomplished reader of his own poetry, a fluent broadcaster, a brilliant raconteur. He revelled in his own voice, but unlike many of whom that can be said, he listened just as attentively.

After meeting William I began to read him, at first

more out of curiosity than a feeling that he was my kind of writer. But from the moment I read the first page of *Turbott Wolfe*, that most authentic and deeply felt of all novels about Africa, written when William was eighteen, I was captivated. In his poem "The Wayzgoose" Roy Campbell observed:

> Plomer, 'twas you who, though a boy in age,
> Awoke a sleepy continent to rage,
> Who dared alone to thrash a craven race
> And hold a mirror to its dirty face.

There came other novels – *Sado, The Case is Altered, Museum Pieces* – each illustrating an aspect of William's intense curiosity about quirks of character and the criminal mind, but for me *Turbott Wolfe* was always the book.

In my inscribed copy of *Turbott Wolfe*, in the edition reissued in 1965 with an introduction by Laurens van der Post, there is a photograph of William, Campbell and van der Post taken on the beach at Sezela, Natal, in 1926. It is a historic picture, linking three of South Africa's most remarkable talents at a time when, virtually unknown, they were combining to produce the literary magazine *Voorslag* (which in Afrikaans means "whiplash"). As van der Post observed in his introduction, some of Campbell's earliest and best poems – "The Serf", "Zulu Girl", "Tristan da Cunha" – could not have been written if it had not been for *Turbott Wolfe*'s opening his eyes to the possibility of writing about South Africa in such a way.

Although William had been born in the Northern Transvaal, he was of English parentage and went to Rugby. I always found it difficult to reconcile the ultra-English figure he now was – and probably always had been – with the Zululand trader and apprentice farmer in Basutoland that I knew he once was. Africa was certainly important to him but it left few detectable claims of the kind that it laid on Campbell and van der Post.

Japan was another matter. Just as Harold Acton seems to have inherited the face and gestures of a mandarin Chinese, so did courtly Japan, to which country William set off from South Africa at the age of twenty-two in company with the twenty-year-old van der Post, seem to have left a kind of dye on him. Van der Post soon travelled on, but William stayed for three years, and had it not been for the rise of Japanese militarism and a sudden craving for European culture, he might have remained indefinitely. In his two autobiographical books *Double Lives* and *At Home*, William practised, as far as his personal life was concerned, a reticence that was entirely in keeping with his general fastidiousness. Probably no one who read *Sado* or these two books of memoirs would finish them ignorant of William's homosexuality, even if they knew nothing of the circumstances of his life. But his method of conveying it, however, was discreet, based on hints, not statements. In his preface to *At Home* William had observed, in relation to T. S. Eliot's remark that "the progress of the artist is a continual extinction of personality", that the word "extinction" had seemed rather strong, "but in charting some of the circumstances in which I had my being after returning to England I have felt less interested in myself than in other persons, places, things, works of art, atmospheres and ideas". Towards the end of his life William wrote in a letter that he never felt candour to be a constant necessity, "if only because people who keep telling one all about themselves, in print or viva voce, are apt to be unduly self-centred, to assume that what is important to them will seem so to others, and therefore to be extremely boring. I think blatant homosexuality, like other forms of blatancy, can be tiresome and uncivilized." It is a fact, too, which more writers of autobiographies should bear in mind, that whereas sexual imagery and descriptions in fiction, art and photography can work effectively because

208

the imagination has come into play, any such details about the narrator's own life fail to work, coming over as boastful, flat and tedious.

Being "civilized" was what William, I think, rated above all. For someone like myself, persuaded at one time that Henry Miller's *Tropics* were autobiography at its most honest and truthful, he was a valuable corrective. Much as I admired and used to enjoy Miller I know whose work I would rather re-read of the two.

William's Sussex, because of his lack of interest in cricket, was not mine, but in other respects it coincided. As a schoolboy he, too, had spent holidays in Eastbourne, when the 1914–18 war was in its last throes but, according to William, gunfire was still audible across the Channel. Like myself William opted out of the school Cadet Corps, in his case through myopia, not distaste. Unlike myself, though, based generally at Ardingly, William had the Downs on his doorstep. It was not surprising, after Africa and Japan, and a quarter of a century in the "murder mile" of Bayswater, that he should return to them.

Yet for one who observed of himself that, despite a sociable nature, he needed domestic insulation and had a taste for simple living, his choice of place seemed perverse. Sussex is not short of pretty country villages, with unpretentious cottages that nevertheless have agreeable gardens and fields to look at, and William could surely have afforded something of the sort. Instead, he seemed actually to prefer the anonymity of the housing estate, almost to revel in its lack of aesthetic appeal. The interior of William's two bungalows was little different from that of any of his neighbours': books were not on show, the pictures were of negligible interest, the furniture was ugly. The pocket-handkerchief gardens were inoffensively neat but devoid of character.

William may have been led to Rustington, the first of his two Sussex establishments, by the fact that his old father, then in his eighties, was installed there. His father died soon after William moved in, but the nearby beach and the local sprawl of market gardens came to please William enough for him to stay there for thirteen years. He now had Charles Erdman in tow, an excitable German exile and a lame dog of the kind attractive to William. Bald and squat, Charles was a former pastrycook acting as a cloakroom attendant, with nowhere to live, when William took him on. The exact nature of their relationship was never quite clear, though presumably it had romantic and sexual origins. When they first moved to Hassocks we always asked Charles with William to any meal, but it soon became clear that William preferred to come by himself. Charles had an engaging side, but he could also be paranoid, and William once remarked jokingly that he sometimes felt like filling Charles's pockets with stones and dropping him off the end of Brighton pier. Yet, in many ways, they were a devoted couple.

William spent ten years in Hassocks and never more than a few weeks passed without his walking over to dinner, usually when John Betjeman was staying, or Cyril or Cuthbert had been invited. We once went to lunch with him and Charles at Adastra Avenue but it was not a success. Charles got worked up and over-anxious about the cooking and his nervousness was infectious. William, whether out of politeness or familiarity, appeared unsurprised by the ruin on his plate.

I would always offer to drive William back after dinner, but regardless of the weather he would insist on walking. His doctor, he said, had recommended a brisk walk last thing, and at military pace he would set off down the lane, stick swinging and cloth cap firmly in place. It was less than a quarter of a mile to the church, after which he would turn right at Clayton tunnel – scene of a historic train disaster in the early days of the century, an event much to William's taste – and take the cinder track that followed the railway line into Hassocks. Years ago, when he was a young man, his mother had looked out of the Brighton train and pointed to the Downs, the windmills above Clayton tunnel and the village folded into the slopes beneath, remarking wistfully to William, "I should have liked to live here, I'd have been happier." William used to cheer Charles up when he was despondent, so he told me, by saying "Hassocks is for Happiness".

Cyril and Cuthbert, though fond enough of William, were not always pleased to find him as a fellow guest, for William was inclined to hold forth, "rattling on" as he put it. Cyril, though increasingly silent as he grew older, preferred a more intimate form of dialogue. William possessed an actor's timing and sense of the melodramatic, and his more florid style tended to make Cyril, himself mimetic and gossipy, shrivel. Betjeman was another matter; he delighted in William's macabre anecdotes and unmalicious tales of misadventure. Both natural life-enhancers, unmoody and uncompetitive, they made life seem wonderfully uncomplicated when they were together.

Of all those, though, who came to dine with us at Clayton when William was present, the one closest in experience to William was James Stern. They shared Africa, both having lived in lonely isolation on the African veld, and having written their first books there. In the piece he contributed to the *London Magazine* after William's death, Jimmy described his first meeting with William: "With his clipped moustache, dark hair brushed back, the thick-lensed horn-rimmed spectacles, the considerate, enquiring, courteous manner, he struck me as a cross between a doctor and an army chaplain with a sense, a surprising sense, of humour." William himself thought he looked like a dentist and indeed one could imagine him, chortling quietly at the impersonation, in a long white jacket.

He liked playing parts and on one occasion had himself photographed lying in an open tomb in Salisbury Cathedral.

William, as I did, collected postcards and we must have exchanged hundreds over the years. The last card I received from him, two weeks before his death, was of a picture called *Ceylon Tea Estate with Pluckers at Work* and on the back William had written, "Very happy to come to you on Saturday, when I've finished my tea-plucking." The last but one had been during a long drought in July and he wrote, "Like the Transvaal, you rightly say, and just think how I have had to keep watering my tiny plot of *Cannabis indica*. There's nothing like that home-grown flavour." I had asked him to review a book about Siegfried Sassoon. He replied:

> I'm sorry to say that the book about Sassoon, which I'd heard about, is one which I think I oughtn't to attempt to review. I think it's about his going Papist, which seems to me outside my scope, and also, though it may have been consistent or inevitable, somewhat depressing, because to my mind the later pious poems are thin stuff . . .
>
> The other day, in a tremendous thunderstorm, I visited the grave of Henry Vaughan with some people. We then shook ourselves like spaniels after a swim, and went inside, where I read Sassoon's "At the Grave of Henry Vaughan". In the church is an eighteenth-century mural tablet to a man called Thynne Gwynne, which I do think a memorable name.

Few letters or cards of William's failed to remark on some such oddity of association. His own ballads – "French Lisette", "The Flying Bum", "Slightly Foxed", "The Dorking Thigh" – are full of them, the horrific and the farcical often inextricably entangled. I myself preferred his beautiful African poems, written "straight". Philip Larkin agreed, declining in a letter to write about William for the *London Magazine*. "I didn't greatly care for his so-called satire poems, but every so often he displayed a vein of feeling that made me wish he would exploit it more often."

The feeling was unmistakably there, though usually masked. William was so various a person, so compartmentalized, that few could come to terms with all of him. He wrote five novels and five volumes of short stories, six collections of poetry, two volumes of memoirs, two biographies (one of Cecil Rhodes) and four librettos for Benjamin Britten. He was quite secretive about his friends, bringing some together but not others; a common enough trait, perhaps.

If there was not all of William in any one book, any one relationship, there was all of him in the sideways inclination of his head, his laugh, his voice. He was meticulous in everything, from the bold writing in violet ink to the phrasing of the most banal remark. Thoughtful and kind as he was, he delighted in the pretensions and small vanities of others. The eyes would glint behind his specs, and the lips, slanted slightly in repose, lift in their pleasure. In him great gravity and scrupulousness of attention trembled on the brink of disregard, both for himself and for humanity in general, in all its absurdity and incongruity. He shared this with his readers and his listeners, and especially with his friends.

One liked to offer him odd happenings by way of return. Once shortly after John Betjeman, who was a godfather to our son, had been made Poet Laureate, we went together to Ardingly College chapel, a building of which John was particularly fond. Unfortunately, when we got there the entrance to the chapel was roped off and marked with a notice stating Strictly No Entry Without Authorization. The school was on holiday and presumably some kind of restoration was going on.

The door, however, was open, and since there appeared to be nobody about we thought we'd risk it. While we were on our way out a huge, black-gowned figure with a white beard spied us from the far end of the cloister. Perhaps suspecting we were making off with the altar silver, he began waving his stick theatrically and shouting.

I was prepared for us to stand our ground and explain our presence. But something got into John, a kind of schoolboy mischievousness, and he whispered "Let's make a run for it." So we set off at full tilt, which immediately set the bearded giant running in pursuit. As we turned the corner we heard a terrific crash, followed by oaths. Fearfully looking back we saw a scatter of gown, stick and whiskers strewn across the protective rope. I regaled William with this story when next I saw him but, inclining his head, he merely nodded quizzically. I thought he was sceptical about its accuracy but it turned out that he had been having tea with the Headmaster and had seen it all.

William was never unkind about his Hassocks neighbours. On the other hand he was happy to poke fun at homosexuals of either sex, such as D'Arcy Honeybunn, "a rose-red sissy half as old as time", and other inhabitants of "Heavenly Mansions, Double you One":

> There you'll encounter aunts of either sex,
> Their jokes equivocal or over-ripe,
> Ambiguous couples wearing slacks and specs
> And the stout lesbian knocking out her pipe.

The last line of this always reminded me of Miss Stobart who lived across the field from us. She was round as a barrel, ruddy as an apple and rarely to be seen without a fag stuck to her lower lip; this was exchanged in the seclusion of her cottage for a variety of pipes. She usually wore a sacking apron, patched trousers and large boots. With Miss Peacock, with whom she shared her life, she raised wonderful vegetables fed from rich stocks of compost. I tried to get her to meet William, for she was a mine of interesting information and noble in manner. Eccentric though she undeniably was she was endearing rather than mockable and William would not have found her otherwise. In her decline – she was of a great age – she unfortunately became reclusive and suspicious in her dealings, to the extent that, when I was rebuilding the banks surrounding the duck pond that bordered both our properties, she refused to let me straighten a one-yard stretch or buy it from her. Instead she put a piece of string across the water, denoting that the adjacent mudpie was still hers. We made peace before she died, I'm glad to say, for she was an original, poetry-loving and pure in heart.

I had better luck in introducing William to another neighbour, Arthur Ashley, not unlike Mollie Stobart in appearance but tiny and male. Arthur had spent most of his early life attached to racing stables, mucking out and doing some riding work. He liked to claim he had risen to become assistant trainer but I think he was boasting. When the war came to an end he moved to Hassocks from the Lambourn area and with his wife, who was as thin as he was round, went into domestic service. When their employer died he started a one-man, one-car taxi service at the station and acquired a council house in the street next to William's. The vehicle was an ancient Rolls, from the outside of which all you could see of Arthur was his peaked cap just astern of the steering wheel. Sometimes, on the rare occasions when William had to go further afield than he could walk, Arthur would drive him. They made a fine sight, like a mayoral procession, with William smiling twistedly like a cat in the back seat. I was happy to have brought them together, for Arthur was the kindliest of souls, always eager to help. He expressed reservations as to the suitability of Charles as a companion for William and enquired from time to time as to whether William had been married.

William died of a heart attack on 21 September 1973, in the same week that Pablo Neruda, who was the same age as William, and Wystan Auden, three years younger, died. It was William's second attack in five days, both of them during what was considered at the time by the oldest inhabitants to have been the worst series of storms in the South Downs this century. William had always refused to have a telephone, a decision that probably cost him his life, since poor Charles had to rush out to find a call box in the middle of the night and predictably the one he found was out of order.

After William's death Charles and I went through the four photograph albums and neatly labelled folders that William kept in a cupboard, to choose illustrations for the articles that James Stern, Paul Bailey, Charles Causley, Ted Walker and Susan Hill were contributing to the *London Magazine* Plomer issue. There was William as a child in Louis Trichardt in the Transvaal, William at prep school and at Rugby; there was William sleek as an otter on the beach at Glyphada in 1930 and at Villefranche five years later; William walking along the front at Dover in 1936 with Joe Ackerley, who is wearing a beret and looking like a French onion man. There was William Japanese-like in Japan and William sitting on a five-barred gate in a Sussex field while Christopher Isherwood and E. M. Forster leant against it.

More recently, there he was in a deck chair alongside Tania Stern at 43 Adastra Avenue and with his arm round his old friend John Morris, one-time mountaineer, author and BBC executive. John Morris had been a Gurkha officer before the war and living in Clayton was a former Gurkha brigadier. When I asked him if he knew John Morris he said, "Which one? There were two Johnny Morrises. I expect your friend was old Bumjaw." He was right, though I didn't like to ask whether the nickname derived from John's facial proportions or his habits. John Morris, incidentally, was not the only famous climber to make regular visits to the neighbourhood, for Miss Stobart's nephew Tom, a large, shambling figure who much resembled her, was the photographer on the successful Everest expedition in Coronation year. Tom Stobart came regularly to Clayton, though he was often abroad leading expeditions to Nepal or the tiger areas of the Hooghly estuary. A fine writer on food and a man of unusual gifts, he was often down on his luck in the latter part of his life, his various schemes and enterprises for making money tending unaccountably to collapse. He keeled over outside Hassocks station on his return from London one day and died on the spot. Arthur Ashley had at the time lost his licence for being found asleep at the wheel, so was not in attendance.

Cyril, Cuthbert, William, closest of my friends and neighbours, and before the decade was out all of them dead. So, too, was Hugh Williams, a frequent visitor with his beautiful wife Margaret. The Williamses, who lived in the shadow of Harold Macmillan at Chelwood Gate, had survived various financial crises, prewar tax debts making life almost impossible until the plays they began to write together baled them out. Their son Hugo was the same age as my stepdaughter Victoria, and their friendship was the first link between our two families. Hugo, his mother's son in looks, never managed to please his father in quite the same way as did his younger brother Simon, but if the relationship had been more harmonious, the evocative and moving poems by which, after his father's death, Hugo sought to repair it would not have been written. "Tam" Williams, after making his name during the '30s in plays such as *While Parents Sleep* and *The Green Bay Tree*, had been swept off to Hollywood, his flourishing career as a film actor interrupted by the war. He had been my sister Daphne's favourite film star during our Eastbourne holidays and been briefly at Haileybury before joining the Liverpool Repertory Theatre at a tender age.

One day in 1937 Frank Vosper, author of *Murder on the Second Floor* and *Love from a Stranger*, had come into the Le Bas junior houseroom at Haileybury. A large, rather alarming-looking figure, he had announced himself as an old Le Bas boy of twenty years earlier, just popping in for a look round. He asked me to tea at the Grubber, and much flattered, for he was equally well known as an actor and playwright at the time, I shared a gargantuan blow-out with him. It had made an impression on me that although he spoke generously, as a fellow Haileyburian, about Hugh Williams, with whom he had acted, he showed no inclination to talk about himself. A few weeks after this meeting took place Frank Vosper was reported to have drowned falling out of a porthole of the SS *Paris* on his way back from America. Considering his huge bulk such a possibility seemed remote. The subsequent press coverage of the affair suggested sexual scandal of a bizarre nature, with allegations of murder that were never substantiated.

Hugo had begun writing poetry at Eton and can only have been sixteen when he showed me, or his mother did, a poem called "Boy at a Cricket Match". It began:

> Holding his hands like strange ivy,
> he twines them round his mother's broad shadow;
> She is his tree, only with her he grows . . .
>
> Turning horizon-smiling eyes around,
> He sees the sky aghast with light
> Between the trees, oppressive boughs, and sees
> The bowler flex his arms like wings
> And knows a real need for flight.

I printed it in *The Cricketer's Companion*, perhaps the least cricket-related poem in the book, but one suggestive enough of a real time and place. A few years later Hugo came to work on the *London Magazine*, while his brother Simon was already about to take the first steps to becoming an actor rather in the style of his father.

Hugh Williams made the most lethal Martinis I have ever encountered, he himself seeming more or less immune to their effects. More than once I ended up in the ditch of their drive, setting off home later at a snail's pace. That Hugo should have come our way was a piece of luck, and though, after his father's death in 1969, the family left Sussex, he continued to come to Clayton until we ourselves departed in 1978, having sold the house and decided amicably to go our own ways. Hugo's cunningly understated poems, in keeping with his own character, have a deceptively innocuous air. He manages, with an apparent minimum of personal involvement, to affect and to amuse. His styles of dressing, living and looking change from time to time, but he remains endearingly the same person as when we used to play squash together at Haywards Heath twenty-five years ago.

Yet, although no longer my home, Sussex has remained almost as powerful a physical presence as before. Jonathan and Victoria had grown up there, and friends from all parts of our life had come to stay: Fullers and Symonses, Hutchinsons and Becketts, Spenders and Powells. The visitors' book bore witness to Leonard Hutton and Keith Miller, to Gavin Ewart and Ian Hamilton, to Derek Walcott and Keith Vaughan, to Leonard Rosoman and Laurie Lee. Also, for me, indelibly associated with Clayton, and a brief survivor of it, was my bearded collie Daisy. The most patient and loyal of creatures, on Fridays she would lie all day in the orchard by the garage until she heard the noise of my car. When I emerged she would rise up on her haunches but remain deliberately in position, her paws marking time, the only visible sign of her awareness. As soon as I called her name she would streak, as if out of a starting stall, through the long grass and, having made contact, execute a series of astonishing vertical leaps. Later, we would set off together through the water garden and, crossing the lane, climb the stile that led into a series of adjoining and open fields.

From here, there were the Downs to the south, an extended green arm cradling the village, and to the north, rising out of woods, the spire of Ditchling church. To the east were fields and hedges looped together under a sea-lightened sky. As if released from some encapsulating dream Daisy would suddenly take off, at first following the contours of the fields, her coat flattened against her body, her muzzle streamlined. For half an hour she would race, a grey blur low to the ground, and then, the frustrations of the week worked out of her, brake to an abrupt halt, sidling back across country, her tongue hanging out. Normal life could be resumed and, until next time, whatever had to be done we could do together.

She eloped once with the farm collie, rather shamefacedly producing five puppies, and another time, frightened in a storm – the same storm in which William died – tore heedlessly through field after field, finally getting caught up in a hedge where she lay trapped for hours. She was skilful at rounding up sheep, anxious to display her prowess, though forbidden; a warning she mutely sought approval to ignore. She came to London at the age of fifteen, rather blind and arthritic, and quite unused to metropolitan living quarters. But she had her more gracious version of fun in Hyde Park and Battersea, and with her and my new family of Liz Claridge, her daughter Lucy and the bearded collie Bella which I had given to Liz some years before, she settled into a matriarchal old age. She had soon to relinquish office-dog duties, taken over by Bella, and in due course, on the most heartbreaking of days, we had to have her put down. But there is still no inch of the Downs above Clayton or the fields below them that I do not see at least partly in terms of her power and beauty and affection. She coloured my life in a quite extraordinary way, a creature of immense dignity as well as humour, and no sufferer of fools.

Bella, equally companionable and engaging, remains a rather more frivolous character, even in what has now become her own old age.

Daisy was not the only animal involved at Clayton. There were once, for example, two cats. Norma was flattened in the lane by the postvan and Sailor, a sulky animal with the nature of a sea lawyer, mercifully took up lodging elsewhere.

More importantly, there were the donkeys. A large, lush field, bordered by ancient beeches and with a stream running along one side of it, separated us from Mollie Stobart's compost heaps and weaving sheds. Mollie's handsome niece Anne, recently arrived in the village, brought with her two donkeys, highly bred but of uncertain temper. Anne was the kind of archetypal country person able to turn her hand to anything to do with animals or plants. When she found it financially difficult to manage the donkeys I went into partnership with her, our intention being to breed in a small way and make the business self-supporting.

Accordingly, we imported new stock of both sexes, lovely fawn and white creatures who greatly enhanced the landscape. A fine new shed was installed under the beeches and there, season by season, foaling took place. Daisy did not altogether take to the donkeys, whose appearance – their huge soft ears in particular – was more rewarding than their character. Donkeys, I came to discover, tend to an offhand manner and a detached temperament. They put up with affection rather than respond to it. Nevertheless, they made an agreeable sight, hock-deep in the long grasses, their delicate legs picking tracks through the buttercups. Sometimes, at their most endearing, they would frolic together, racing at the sunset or duffing one another up.

We sold the progeny from time to time, including one handsome fellow to Mai and David Hughes, then setting up home in southern France. His amorous attacks on Mai forced them eventually to pass him on, but lecherous habits were no drawback in the film industry and he made a name for himself in lusty dramas involving Provençal peasantry.

Donkeys, though they may appear less fragile than race-horses, are equally prey to infirmities of bone, skin and intestine. The toes of our lot became an endless source of worry and expense, requiring more frequent chiropody than the most corn-encrusted dowager. As the charm wore off, so did the cost of keeping them increase. Customers for new arrivals became less easy to find and it began to seem as if we would soon be surrounded by a whole herd of donkeys, the dusk shattered by their melancholy tribal baying. Reluctantly, but with some relief too, we abandoned the enterprise as a business, running it down until it reverted to Anne's original holding.

Donkeys at Dusk

All day they had stood in the heat
Like statues, immune to weather
Or flies, but occasionally towing
Dusty effigies to new moorings.

Then, in the cool,
Powdery bodies striped with sunset,
They seemed to lose patience,
Charging like zebra for water.
And, as suddenly, stopped,
Atavism gone out of them,
The stream reflecting their manes,
Clouds racing to dispersal.

Yearlings

A string of horses black against the snow,
December light already beginning to go

And the beeches absorbing them, a rust
Tunnel through whose leafless crust

They trot, shadowy invaders.
Caparisoned, they suggest courtliness

And lineage, heirs
To historic names whose sires

Look on through hooded eyes,
Innocent yet of pride or surprise.

Before Racing

Pink layer of icing sugar,
Till the straw sun dissolves it,
And the Downs, drained by the cold
Of their green, sweep grey
To grey sea. Trees are mastheads.

Elements of blue like eyelids,
Open sky clinking iron,
With hooves of horses on bridle
Paths, back after riding out,
And the lanes lathered with breath.

As yet it is anybody's
Morning, a slate clouded
With nothing; but gradually,
Under the cold, something's
Moving, beginning to conspire
Towards a finish flushed with silver.

Instead of a Drawing

At this moment I want no more
Than that I could transmit a likeness
On to paper, taking this pencil
Into my confidence; set you in dress –
Ribbed jersey, flared skirt, thin bangles –
Or undress, light on all the planes
And angles that go to make a body
Taste and smell and look just so –
With the certainty that on this page
Drawing reinstated the image.

Grand Canal

Your hair that makes the most of vines,
Blue shirt against the trellis, and goggles,
Like insect's eyes, reflecting the lagoon.

That's all the Kodacolor yields,
To which I add a table
Where Negronis glint, a liquid air

That melts between viewfinder and the view.
The lap of gondolas, of subdued jazz,
Great domes that nudge the sun,

The biscuit palaces, exist without,
Beyond the edges of the fading print.
It was a time of meeting elsewhere soon,

Of brief goodbyes in golden afternoon.
I look again and feel the first
Faint smears of rust in autumn's deadly tune.

Goodbye in Rome

Gone, and in my driving mirror
The taxi rattles you from sight.
Already I experience symptoms
Of withdrawal, the terror
Separation flies like a kite.

Under a sky etched out in inks,
Dark urine and rose, a fidget
Of wind flaps girls' skirts,
– An image that hurts –
Ripples white shirts.

Past Piazza Navona, heading south
Towards Gaeta, I drive
With hood down, my mouth
Tasting dusty, of your mouth
And ashes. Like being buried alive.

Beyond Naples

And even here in the south
Where resentment shapes the mouth
Like a lipstick and the baring
Of full breasts under black cotton
Holds a tenderness akin to swearing
– the harsh syllables sluiced with spit –
Poverty has a style, *un perfetto bilico*,
Adherents recognize, dying from lack of it.

PART VII

The Racing Game

BY THIS TIME, TOO, I had acquired a new interest. For most of
my adult life I have backed horses, usually one or two a day,
for modest sums. I have had my share of winning streaks,
though in the long run I have, I suppose, lost, like everyone
else. The sums were inconsiderable either way; just enough to
effect a change of mood, up or down.

Sometime in 1965, at an *Observer* lunch, I casually enquired
of John Hislop, our racing correspondent, about the costs of
owning a racehorse. Training fees, with a small rather than
fashionable trainer, were then about eleven pounds a week,
and, according to John, you could with luck acquire a jumper
good enough to have fun with for about six hundred pounds.

The outlay for training did not seem greatly in excess of
what, if I was realistic, gambling was already costing me and,
of course, if the animal proved to be any good, there would be
prize money coming back. John made it clear that many
racehorse owners never have a winner in their lives and others
have to wait years before striking lucky. He recommended
that, if I was serious about it, I should start modestly and with
a trainer making his way. There was one such, he continued,
in Ditchling, a former steeplechase jockey who had been
obliged to retire after a bad injury. His name was Alan
Oughton and he had only just obtained his licence.

229

I brooded on all this, on the probable outlay and running costs. In Australia, when I was there for the *Observer* in 1954–5, I had bought for very little money a number of contemporary paintings – by Drysdale, Nolan, Boyd, Daws among others – and in the ten years since they had greatly increased in value. I thought I should try and make racing work by exchanging pictures for horses, one at a time, as necessary, and never paying more for a horse than I had got for a picture.

So one day, after consultation with Alan Oughton, I sold a painting by Lawrence Daws for £600 and bought for the same sum a three-year-old grey gelding called Acrovat, by the 1955 Derby favourite Acropolis. Beautifully bred by Donatello out of a Hyperion mare, Acropolis had finished third in that race, but later won the Voltigeur Stakes at York. Despite his immaculate pedigree, Acrovat was not physically impressive, even to my untutored and doting eye. In fact, small, lean, short-legged and grizzled, he looked like a scoundrel, not at all what you would expect of the progeny of a classic, liver-coloured chestnut. He had run a few times on the flat, picking up a small race in Bath, but Alan Oughton was a trainer of jumpers and we were proposing to run him over hurdles.

I went over as soon as I could to see him at Findon, a downland village north of Worthing, where Alan had just taken over a small yard. Alan had been a successful rider over fences, once finishing third in the Grand National, and to start him off a few owners for whom he had ridden winners had sent him horses to train. The son of a Portsmouth tailor, he had begun riding during his National Service in the Veterinary Corps and, despite being over six feet tall, had been able to turn professional with fair results.

This was starting about as humbly as you could: a cheap horse, who had failed to fetch his reserve at Ascot sales, and an inexperienced trainer. But at least I was in; the fever first contracted all those years ago in Calcutta, when at the age of six I had accompanied my father to that most beautiful of racecourses alongside the Hooghly, was about to be assuaged, or so I hoped. The layout and buildings of the Royal Calcutta Turf Club had remained throughout the intervening thirty-five years as vivid to me as in a painting: the sweep of Chowringhee from the stands, the glint of the Hooghly bridge, the sails and dhows off the Esplanade, and, under the palm, neem and banyan trees that lined the paddock and the course itself, the glossy, polished horses, the pink and turquoise of saris, the white-suited men with their cigars and solar topis. The rattle of bridles, the mixed aromas of smoke, dung and horses' sweat, the sickly attars of jasmine and carnation floating down from the private boxes of European grandees and maharajahs, had become so much part of what I remembered of my childhood that it was as if I had never left.

But that was a world and half a lifetime away. Now it would be different.

Meanwhile, there were pleasant enough matters to decide: racing colours, for instance. My first few choices were disallowed. Most single colours and conceivable combinations of colours had already been claimed, which was hardly surprising since registered owners must run into the thousands. Eventually, I was allowed the colours of the current month's *London Magazine*, brown and pink, the waistcoat brown, the sleeves pink.

Initial results were not encouraging. Acrovat ran, at about three-week intervals, at Plumpton, Windsor and Wye, finishing in mid division twice and on the third occasion last in a field of twenty-eight. He was usually in the lead or well placed until halfway and then, like an old sweat, gradually dropped himself out. In March Acrovat had his fourth race, at Stratford, and finished fourth out of fourteen. That was better, and a fortnight later he was fifth out of twenty-two at Plumpton. His manner of racing, however, was that of one who did not want to exert himself more than necessary, yet did not wish to be disgraced and therefore disposed of. It was a familiar type to anyone who had been in the services.

Acrovat ran three times more that season, his best performance being to finish third out of thirteen in an April quagmire at Plumpton. Andrew Turnell rode him and the sight of his number going up in the frame and his name actually in the papers was something that warmed me all summer. Third prize was £40 and I had backed him for a place at 10–1 – my first week's profit on him. In May Acrovat was turned out and sometimes at weekends I would drive over from Clayton or Hove and watch him munching his way round his paddock under the Downs. He came back into training in early July, looking a lot stronger and more relaxed than when I had bought him.

Still, I was not sure he was going to be worth keeping, nor was Alan Oughton. He had the ability, that was plain, but he did not look as if his heart was in it. For my part, although I did not want to give up so soon, there was no point in persevering with an animal who was never going to give of his best. We decided to run him for a month or so on the firm September ground he liked and, if he showed no more zest for running a race out, send him to one of the autumn sales at Ascot.

The threat of dismissal did wonders for Acrovat, as it was to do again later in his career. In his first race of the new season, at Fontwell in September, he led from start to finish, winning by eight lengths. He had started at 8–1, the outsider of six, and Josh Gifford, the champion jockey who usually rode for Alan's near neighbour, Ryan Price, rode him. A week later, on equally firm going at Plumpton, Acrovat came out again and was never headed. In one week he had paid for a year's training and had something in hand.

The weather broke now and we thought that, with the ground easing and the better-class horses coming in, Acrovat's little run of success would be halted. But it was not. On 31

October, again at Plumpton and in a quality field of fifteen, including several winners, he romped home, jumping beautifully. Again Josh rode him and again he had his nose in front all the way.

It was a magical autumn, and the details of weather were more relevant to me than they had been since the war. The trees turned rusty against the skyline at Plumpton and at Fontwell the paddocks thickened underfoot with fallen leaves. I had never kept a journal but now I began to record each race, and Acrovat's wellbeing, meticulously. I pasted in cuttings and photographs, and if I want to check up on anything which occurred over the subsequent twenty years the clues are more likely to be found in my race books than anywhere else.

Of course, it was too good to last indefinitely. We gave Acrovat a breather and then, when he was ready to run again, the frosts came and racing was cancelled. Throughout January and February the going was appalling and for a small horse like him a hopeless proposition. It never really improved, and though Acrovat ran gamely enough, finishing third once in a big field at Folkestone, he never again looked like winning. The fact that Josh Gifford was usually riding against us for Ryan Price also made a difference.

Acrovat began the next season with three thirds in a row, each time in large fields. Foot-and-mouth disease halted racing in midwinter for six weeks and when it began again Acrovat showed little enthusiasm for it. He ran several times unplaced, coming in to be unsaddled with a furtive and slightly guilty air, as if conscious that he could have done better.

Then, on a freezing March day at Lingfield, in by far the most valuable and difficult race of his season, he took it upon himself to upset the form. The favourite, Orator, fell two out and Acrovat worked his way to the front to win on the post. He had started at 25–1, so he wiped out all previous losses and, with his future again in the balance, redeemed himself just in time.

We thought now that, with the ground drying out, we might have some more fun with him. But he ran three mulish races in succession, making virtually no show. Typically, then, when confidence in him was at low ebb and his price was drifting from favourite to outsider, he ran a blinder on the very last day of the season, getting up to win a good race in the last stride.

Acrovat was turned out now, but although I kept him another eighteen months that was the last of his jokes. He ran ten times the next season and was never placed. Arthur Ashley, who had taken to accompanying me to the races, was greatly disapproving of my loyalty to the old horse. "Never get married to them," he used to say, his off-duty flat cap low over his eyes, a fag forever on his lip, so that he looked more like Andy Capp than ever. I never exactly felt married to Acrovat but I did feel loyal to him. He had given me my first taste of racing as an owner and if the triumphs had come at long intervals they had nevertheless outweighed the disappointments. I let him have one more summer at grass and then ran him until Christmas. He was second once, just before the Ascot sales. But it was too late. I got exactly what I had paid for him, so he owed me almost nothing.

Arthur meanwhile had become ambitious on my behalf. "Come on now," he said, "let's jump in with both feet." By this he meant that I should shift some more of what seemed to him incomprehensible scrawls from my walls and get a decent horse. Despite his puny presence Acrovat had won five races, but Arthur now wanted us to have a good-looking horse, something a bit up the social scale. He had become so dictatorial to Alan Oughton in the paddock that, to keep the peace, I had to resort to sending him on scouting operations among the bookmakers. Allowed into the paddock with me he would lay down the law to the jockey before Alan could get a word in.

I had now got the feel of the business, begun to know the

courses and the jockeys, and the way different horses should be ridden. I read the form book every night, more conscientiously than I had ever read Wisden, and I studied breeding. Placing horses cleverly, especially the more moderate ones, is half the battle, and before we decided to run anywhere I went over the likely opposition with a microscope. This naturally did not guarantee that Acrovat would win, but it did mean that he ran where he was best handicapped and on courses and going that suited him. What he taught me, rapidly and emphatically, was that horses have characters and moods, and that in racing nothing can be taken for granted.

Racehorses are made of glass, Lester Piggott once said, and it is true. Keeping them sound is the hardest part. In that respect Acrovat proved to be one of my luckiest horses. His only period off the course was early on. A milk cart startled him coming off the Downs one morning and he threw the boy riding him, careering down the lane and across the Worthing road, narrowly missing the traffic. He ended up in a hedge with nothing worse than scratches and a sprained foot.

Egged on by Ashley I sold another picture in the autumn of 1968, at a better price than I had expected, as a result of which I arranged for Alan Oughton to go over to Brian Swift's yard at Epsom where there was a three-year-old Zarathustra gelding called Zaras Pearl for sale. Swift had another three-year-old, Blameless Stall, also on offer, the asking price for the pair being slightly over what I had got for my picture. Zaras Pearl had only run once, but Blameless Stall, by Above Suspicion out of Caledonian Market, had won twice during the preceding season on the flat.

Alan Oughton liked them equally, and greatly daring, intending to keep whichever proved best and resell the other, I bought both. Ashley, when I took him over to Findon to inspect them, approved of Zaras Pearl but forcibly expressed the view that Blameless Stall was a waste of money and should be passed on immediately.

As it happened they both proved an investment, Blameless winning six races and Zaras four, including the valuable Carta Carna trophy at Folkestone. Neither found his form at once and when, after four races each, neither had been placed, I began to get worried. "Get rid of them," Arthur advised, forgetting how much Zaras Pearl's breeding and conformation had appealed to him. Then, right at the end of the season, Blameless won at Plumpton and Zaras started to look like something.

Both were more reliable than Acrovat but they were totally different, from him and from each other, in temperament and style of racing. Blameless, we were to discover, liked only two racecourses, Plumpton and Worcester. He won five times at Plumpton and once at Worcester and was rarely out of the first three at either. He plodded dozily round the paddock before the race and for two-thirds of it he ran as if he was totally asleep. Time after time he appeared to have no chance, lethargically tagging along at the rear of the field. Then, with the stables in sight and only two or three hurdles left to jump, he would suddenly wake up, appear to realize what he was there for and eat up the ground. In the winner's enclosure he gazed about nonchalantly, as if surprised anyone should doubt his capacity. Away from Plumpton and Worcester – at Cheltenham, Sandown, Kempton – he made no effort whatsoever, and when eventually we put him to jumping fences he glared balefully at them and ground to a halt.

Zaras Pearl was as highly strung as Blameless was sluggish. He trembled when he was being saddled, rolling his eyes apprehensively at the approach of the jockeys. Never a brave horse, he usually ran spiritedly and consistently once he had settled in and we were not, as we were with Blameless, restricted to just two courses.

All the same, Blameless had won four times before Zaras, after a sequence of seconds and thirds, got his nose in front. Zaras' first and most valuable win was a strange affair. We had run him in a small race at Towcester one November

Saturday, thinking he had a good chance, since he had several times been second in good company. He ran very disappointingly, finishing a bad third out of four runners. On the way back I began to read a biography of Captain Boyd-Rochfort, who had trained Zaras Pearl's sire, Zarathustra, winner at the age of six of the Ascot Gold Cup. Boyd-Rochfort was quoted as saying that Zarathustra always ran best when he had two races in abnormally quick succession.

On the Sunday morning I rang Alan Oughton to discover how Zaras Pearl had come out of his race. Alan said that he was kicking and squealing and generally behaving as if he badly needed a race, not at all like a horse that had just had one and travelled several hundred miles as well. I told Alan what I had learned about Zarathustra and suggested, expecting not to be taken seriously, that we run him in the big race at Folkestone the next day. He was already declared for that but, since it was a highly competitive affair and we wanted a result from him, we had chosen the Towcester race instead. To my surprise Alan agreed, saying he couldn't run any worse than he had at Towcester and since we had paid the entry fee there was nothing to be lost.

Ashley drove to Folkestone with me, insisting that he was only coming because there was a horse he wanted to back in another race. He smirked condescendingly at the idea of running Zaras so soon. "There's a dozen that could beat him even if he had been laid out specially."

On the way we got a puncture and I made Ashley change the wheel as a punishment for his gloomy grumbling. We arrived on a misty afternoon just as the jockeys for our race were entering the paddock. I steered Ashley away from it and told him to go and put a fiver on for me at the best price he could get. He padded off, muttering he supposed he'd better put something on himself, since the horse was at such long odds and he didn't like to see him run "friendless", as he put it.

John Jenkins, who had ridden Zaras in his last few races, was told to let the horse enjoy himself but to try and keep him covered up for as long as possible. This he did, bringing him to the outside as they turned into the straight. We expected that Zaras would now fold up, but to our astonishment and delight he picked up the horses in front of him one by one and at the last hurdle jumped into the lead. He was pressed all the way to the line by the two favourites but just held on.

In contrast to his performance at Towcester he came in fresh as a daisy. Ashley arrived at the winner's enclosure, grinning all over his face and saying that he always thought Folkestone was the course for Zaras and two and a half miles, not two miles – as at Towcester – his correct trip. He had got 16–1 for us both and he had put £10 on for himself.

The prize money was £1100, a lot of money for a hurdle race in 1970, and an inscribed silver cigarette box, in front of me as I write this, came with it. Ashley put half his winnings on the horse he had allegedly come to back and it finished last, which was just as well, for otherwise he would have been intolerable on the journey home. After Zaras Pearl's Carta Carna win Blameless was put on his mettle, romping in at Plumpton to pick up the valuable Mark Lane Handicap, which came with a silver tankard.

The fairly consistent success, at a decent level, that now came our way was marred by the sudden death from cancer of Alan Oughton. He had came back from a summer holiday in Corfu with what was originally diagnosed as sinus trouble and by the next summer, after a series of operations, he was dead. It was a difficult time for his family, for they were just beginning to build a reputation and to find new owners. Luckily Alan's widow, Diane, was bred to the game. Her brother, Bill Rees, had been a top jump jockey, who was retained by Peter Cazalet and rode all the Queen Mother's National Hunt horses until his recent retirement. He had, in fact, ridden Blameless Stall to his first two wins. Their father and uncle were legendary jockeys of the early '20s, who each rode the winner of the Champion Hurdle, the Cheltenham Gold Cup and the Grand National, a unique record.

In the following season Zaras Pearl won twice in succession and was hardly ever out of the first three. Blameless won once more and then developed leg trouble. I sold them both in June 1973, Blameless for 500 guineas and Zaras for 1500 guineas; they had both paid their way in pleasure, if not quite in prize money, several times over.

With the money received I bought a handsome unbroken three-year-old gelding, bred in Ireland. He was of pure jumping stock, being by the hurdler Harwell out of Muslin, and on the dam's side tracing back to the Cheltenham Gold Cup winner Linwell. We called him Harvest and he proved qualitatively, if not quantitatively, to be my best horse. Unfortunately he broke down at Ascot in only his fourth race and was off the course for eighteen months. When he returned he won three good steeple-chases in his first season, once at Newbury and twice at Lingfield, in company of a higher class than anything Acrovat, Zaras and Blameless had ever faced. He won once more and then broke down again, this time for good. He was a most striking and honest animal, a faultless jumper, and had he remained sound there is no knowing what he might have done.

By now Ashley had appointed himself my racing manager. Usually I drove him in my Citroën; occasionally we went in his Rolls. We set out in all weathers and all seasons, except high summer. We talked about nothing but racing, because his views on everything else were repetitive and odious. Yet he had a heart of gold and there was nothing he would not do for anyone in the village, often driving old people for nothing. Maddening though he could be in his knowingness when talking to trainers and jockeys he really did understand the preparation of horses, and he had many entertaining, if frequently unlikely, stories about betting coups pulled off when he was so-called assistant to "the Commander".

While Harvest was out of action following his first break-down, Arthur expressed the opinion that we should move into flat racing. "You don't want to have your horses trained by a woman," was his usual approach. "It's time you got yourself a proper trainer." I was anxious that Diane Oughton should not be left in the lurch after Alan's death, particularly as some of her owners had already moved to other stables, so not only did I disregard Arthur's advice but I sold another picture and asked Diane to find me something modest to tide us over until Harvest was ready to run again.

She went up to Doncaster sales and returned with a three-year-old called Ragged Robin, previously trained by Peter Walwyn. He was a small, compact creature who had been highly thought of as a yearling but had never lived up to his home reputation on the course.

Josh Gifford had retired now but we had access to the future champion jockey Graham Thorner, who had twice won for me on Zaras Pearl. Graham schooled Ragged Robin and when he seemed to be jumping fluently enough we decided to run him at Taunton. In an eighteen-runner race he got up in the last stride to win by a head. This was an exciting start but my visions of owning a Cheltenham contender were soon shattered. In his next run at Wincanton, with the race at his mercy, he suddenly went in the near fore, Graham immediately pulling him up and dismounting. The tendon had to be split four days later, and there was no question of his racing again for at least a year. In fact, he never fully recovered and though I kept him until he could start work again he was not the same horse. He ran twice and then the same leg went and he had to be put down.

It was at this stage, with Harvest and Ragged Robin both invalids, that Arthur's persistence bore fruit. I had met Gordon Smyth some years earlier at Arundel where he was trainer to the Duke of Norfolk. He was a regular visitor to Hove to watch Sussex and was a useful cricketer himself. We both played for the Sussex Martlets, though never, I think, together. In 1961 Gordon had succeeded his father Willie at Arundel after an apprenticeship of fifteen years, but after falling out with the Duchess in 1965 he left to set up on his own at Lewes. In his first season he trained Lady Zia Wernher's Charlottown to win the Derby.

At that time, since I was on the county cricket committee, I spent most of my summer free time at Hove. Very often I sat with Gordon. I had always regarded flat racing as altogether too grand and expensive an affair for me to get involved in, but Gordon persuaded me that there was far less chance of horses breaking down on the flat, that they need cost no more, and that though his training fees would be higher than the Oughtons', the prize money was higher too.

I was beginning to get withdrawal symptoms now that both my jumpers had been inactive for a long period, so I said to Gordon that if he really thought it could work out I'd like to have a go. "I can't guarantee you success right away," he said, "but I would be very surprised if out of two horses one of them did not come good and pay for the other."

At the next October Newmarket sales Gordon purchased for me a beautiful bay filly by Fabergé for 1750 guineas. I called her Cigarette Case and in her first season she was second twice. A year later, in Dublin, I bought a brown, almost black filly by the champion miler Paveh, whom I named Parvati. She cost twice as much.

I raced both of them for three seasons, during two of which they overlapped. Arthur and I went to Salisbury and Beverley, to Chester and Lingfield, to Newbury and Doncaster, discussing their development as we drove back on long summer evenings. I forbade him the paddock, but he was at home on flat courses and trotted off happily making his own bets. He was respectful to Gordon and wary of him as a real professional. After all, someone who had trained the winner of the Derby was scarcely to be sneezed at, even by an ex-Head Lad.

241

On Sunday mornings I would drive over to Lewes to see Gordon and have a word with my two precious creatures. Cigarette Case was the bright-eyed looker of the two, head high and neck arched, with a white blaze. Parvati was less demonstrative, almost meditative and phlegmatic in comparison, but with an honest, dignified regard. They were as different from each other as Zaras and Blameless had been, and compared with those two they looked tiny.

Gordon's forecast turned out to have been overmodest, for after a quiet start in both cases they not only provided continuous interest but proved wonderful investments. Fillies are rarely raced for more than two or three seasons before going to stud, and by the time Cigarette Case had finished she had won four times and been placed eleven times, while Parvati had won three times and been placed twelve times. Cigarette Case won her last two races, both at Newbury, and Parvati was much fancied for and ran in the Cesarewitch at the end of a season in which she had won the White Horse Stakes at Newbury, run fourteen times and only been out of the first three in her first two races and her last.

When the time came I could scarcely bear to part with them, feeling like a traitor as I watched them walk round the sales ring. Both sold well, Cigarette Case making 9000 guineas, Parvati 7000, and at stud they regularly produced winners, though none outstanding.

They had quite different styles of racing. Cigarette Case could be ridden by any jockey and put anywhere in the field. She would quickly take up the position she wanted, just behind the leaders, and when asked showed real finishing speed. Her best distance was ten furlongs. Parvati was bred to stay on the dam's side and in the end needed two miles. She was inclined to idle early on and needed a strong jockey to keep her in touch. After about a mile and a half she would start to move, coming with a long, sustained run in the straight, like an ocean roller before it breaks.

At one time or another virtually every top jockey of the day, except for Lester Piggott, rode for me – Pat Eddery, Frankie Durr, Willie Carson, Bill Williamson, Edward Hide, Paul Cook, Philip Waldron. Willie Carson, with his driving style, got the best out of Parvati, and if I wanted someone to ride for my life it would be him. It was fascinating to observe the jockeys' various methods and characters – some, like Carson, always optimistic and joking; others, like the Australian Bill Williamson or Greville Starkey, as if at a funeral. Williamson, like Starkey, had a laconic, dry humour, but to look at him you would not think it.

The winter jumping game at small tracks like Plumpton and Fontwell began to seem, in comparison, a cosy, family affair. The prize money, for jockeys, trainers and owners alike, was rarely comparable. I still preferred the atmosphere of National Hunt racing, for it was friendlier and the courses were usually in proper country, but so long as I had Cigarette Case and Parvati there was no course that did not hold out the prospect of a thrilling afternoon.

Arthur Ashley, less condescending these days about my horses, had taken a great fancy to Parvati, and during her first season as a two-year-old, when sixth was the best she could do, he remained faithful to her. "You'll see, next summer," he repeated over and over again, "you just wait." He had his reward, for when Parvati won her first race as a three-year-old she started at 20–1. Arthur had £100 on her, and for weeks he went around treading on air. William Plomer was regaled with every detail of her running every time Arthur drove him. Despite his farming days in the Transvaal, I don't think William was much attuned to racing or animal life in general, but he would have listened politely.

The year after Parvati had been sold Gordon Smyth's yard hit a bad streak. From being one of the top trainers in the country, regularly winning forty to fifty races a year, he went down, for no really explicable reasons, to single figures within

243

a few years. His richer owners began to leave for other trainers or, like Lady Zia Wernher, had died, and even Albert Finney, one of his earliest and most loyal clients, gave up temporarily. Gordon remained much the same, rarely put out by events or losing his composure, perhaps as happy to play golf or watch cricket as train horses, but thoroughly experienced in every aspect of the business.

In 1976 he left for Hong Kong, there to start a new career as trainer to the Royal Hong Kong Jockey Club. I had one more horse with Gordon before he left, a chestnut filly with a lovely blonde tail. She was by the Italian stallion Don out of Avon Star and we called her Star Pupil. If looks had been anything to go by she would have been a champion, but her mind and heart were never in it. She was second early on in a large field at Salisbury as a two-year-old, promising great things, only to fold up in race after race after getting into a winning position. She won once, at Beverley as a three-year-old, but that was her only reward in a dozen races.

After Gordon Smyth had gone I had no incentive, nor any money, to buy another yearling. Star Pupil had wiped out the profits from Cigarette Case and Parvati and herself fetched only 700 guineas, a seventh of what she had cost.

There was another reason. Arthur Ashley's wife had died a few years earlier and his grief had been painful to watch. All the wind and bombast went out of him, and physically, too, he began to shrink. Whereas earlier I could do nothing to prevent him from coming racing, in the end I had to force him, simply to stop him moping and to get him out of his house. He gave up his taxi work, scarcely bothered to read the *Sporting Life*, once never out of his pocket, and took less and less trouble with the cleaning of his bungalow and the garden.

His sight began to go and he had a mild stroke. There was eventually nothing for it but the old people's home in Hassocks, since clearly he could no longer look after himself. He was not happy there, finding no congenial racing company, no one to tell his tales to. I took him for drives when I could but he often seemed confused and anxious, as if he would get into trouble should we be late back. The last time I saw him he was with another inmate, feeling his way along a flint wall, tapping his stick. I called out to him from my car window but he did not hear me. A few days later he was dead. The heady, argumentative drives back from Folkestone and Windsor, from Lingfield and Salisbury, seemed to belong to another age.

For the next ten years I took only a modest interest in racing, rarely going to a meeting. I gambled once a week, on Saturdays, on the races that were televised. Instead, as some kind of therapy, I worked on an anthology to be called *The Turf*, for the Oxford University Press, an undertaking that obliged me to hunt out extracts from the diaries of Charles Greville, Samuel Pepys and John Evelyn, from the novels of Dickens, Surtees, Nat Gould and Hemingway, from the autobiographies of racing writers like George Lambton and Jack Leach. I familiarized myself with the history of the thoroughbred, from the Darley Arabian and Eclipse to great postwar horses like Mill Reef and Brigadier Gerard, and with such Jockey Club stalwarts and rule-makers as Sir Charles Bunbury, Lord George Bentinck and Admiral Rous, the famous handicapper. I read up on bookmakers and old-time jockeys, and collected relevant poems by Ezra Pound, John Betjeman and Philip Larkin, as well as old favourites like "Banjo" Patterson.

"Racing", wrote Charles Greville, who was not only a diarist of renown but the incredibly lucky owner of the classic winners Preserve and Mango out of the same mare, "is just like dram-drinking; momentary excitement and wretched intervals; full consciousness of the mischievous effects of the habit and equal difficulty in abstaining from it." George Moore in *Esther Waters* put it another way: "Henceforth something to live for. Each morning bringing news of the horse, and the hours of the afternoon passing pleasantly, full of thoughts of the evening paper and the gossip of the bar. A bet on a race brings hope into lives which otherwise would be hopeless."

For all its disappointments, the fascination of racing when things are going well is irresistible. When you are actively involved, it colours the whole of life, both in anticipation and in reflection. If the race itself was the whole of it, a matter of a few minutes, then it would certainly not be worth the candle. In any case the nervous anxiety before the start of a race, especially over fences, is a lot more disagreeable than pleasurable. But the racehorse you own, whether acquired as foal or yearling, or three years old, and then followed through its adolescent ups and downs into adult racing life, becomes an extension of the family and you feel as protective towards it as towards a child. Similarly, you can, against the evidence, continue to make excuses for it.

In racing, too, as in cricket, there is a peculiarly English relationship between sport and place. At one time I had driven all over England in an attempt to set cricket in its social and geographical contexts. Now, driving all over the country with Arthur Ashley, I had the chance to do the same with racing. I don't know whether the beauty of the racing game, as opposed to its techniques and manipulation of expertise and chance, ever made much impact on Arthur, but you would have had to be blind and flint-hearted not to have been moved by the spectacle; not just by the lush surroundings, the silks and the bustle, but by the nobility of effort.

The Sussex courses – Goodwood, Fontwell, Plumpton and Brighton – were on our doorstep, but only racing would have taken me to Newbury and Newmarket, Chepstow and Doncaster, Towcester and Cheltenham, Beverley and Taunton, Wolverhampton and Leicester. These places had not been on my cricket circuit.

I found racing an education in many things. Not only did it get me out of London in all weathers and all seasons, when I might not otherwise have budged, but it gave me an interest totally remote from everything else I did, bringing a quite different world, with its own language and disciplines, into focus. The gradual recognition of hitherto unfamiliar skills – the silken touch of some jockeys, the perfect balance, judgement of pace and timing of others – added a new dimension to everyday life. I became a student again.

During the time I was editing Andrew Devonshire's book about his celebrated mare Park Top, which we published with some success, he and I had many discussions in which we tried to analyse exactly what made a race such an affecting and memorable spectacle. It is something difficult to put into words. The pitfalls are so numerous, the horses so vulnerable, that getting them to the course fit and ready to race seems an achievement enough in itself. When they run their hearts out on your behalf and win a race – in my case usually against horses that cost ten or twenty times as much – it is impossible not to be touched and exhilarated.

During the years I had racehorses I spent hundreds of hours trying to translate something of their movement into poetry; not so much racecourse activity but horses at work, their action – as in successive photographs by Muybridge – at various speeds. Some of the results I included in *Blindfold Games*.

There was no shortage of paintings on the subject, reproductions of which I had long been collecting. My favourite of all was Magritte's surrealist *L'Enfance d'Icare*, but in the search for an ideal, composite image, I had made a montage of paintings by Sironi and Dufy, Frith and Géricault, David Jones and Gaudier-Brzeska, Toulouse-Lautrec and Degas, Stubbs and Herring. My best bit of luck was when I came across a 1949 Victor Pasmore, in which a newspaper cutting, listing the runners at Catterick, formed the basis of a lyrical and evocative abstract. This, I felt, was one way that contemporary art, by using a modern idiom, could treat a traditional subject, one handled by great artists of each generation. Could a modern poem achieve the same effect?

247

With Ben Nicholson I began a long correspondence about the drawings of racehorses which he had begun to make on the Yorkshire moors and which I later reproduced in the *London Magazine*. Ben was a prolific letter writer on topics that interested him, particularly those related to sport and design. He liked to evolve elaborate theories about how tennis- and cricket-playing tactics could be improved, and took a childlike pleasure in sports cars. He once invited me to visit him in his Swiss hide-out, above the lake of Brissago, to inspect his gold Renault Floride, a replacement for an earlier Mercedes. "If only some of our sculptors", he wrote on the invitation, "could make a form as good as this (or as the old Alpine Sunbeam) all would be well." I took him up on the invitation, finding myself in the neighbourhood, only to discover him at work on what he said was his annual drawing of an apple, an exercise he conducted as a means of keeping his draughtsman's hand in. He soon put this down and hurried me out to the garage to admire his new toy. It was indeed beautiful, but unfortunately it never occurred to Ben – since he was teetotal and ate fussily – that after a long drive one might need refreshment.

Abstract poems are rarely successful, tending to operate only on one level. I had in the end to do my best with words.

My concern to write a successful racehorse poem may have been partly an attempt to salve my conscience, but it also related to a wish to deal with "popular" subjects sophisticatedly: the reverse of the populist approach. It was, needless to say, no way to popularity; those likely to be attracted by the subject matter were unlikely to be able to respond to anything other than traditional forms. I had, however, long had the idea that certain pictorial techniques, most particularly those of cubist and abstract art, could be used to produce poems that had visual impact, that were in fact a fusion of the two arts, as in the poems of Apollinaire. It was what had attracted me in the first place to concrete poetry, an art that enjoyed only a brief period of interest but which, especially in the hands of Ian Hamilton Finlay, Claus Bremer and Eugen Gomringer, created some indelible images and introduced another dimension into poetry. Like surrealism it was more relevant for its effect and influence, its rejuvenating freshness, than for any sustained period of achievement.

Star Pupil on the flat and Harvest over jumps were not quite my final attachments to racing. One November evening in 1983 David Oughton, Alan and Diane's son, who had lately taken over from his mother, rang me out of the blue to ask if I might be interested in another horse. David's specific reason for contacting me was that one of his owners, a stockbroker, had suddenly been made redundant. He had two children at school and his wife had insisted that the first thing he did must be to sell the steeplechaser he had in training. David, egged on by a former colleague of mine in the press box, and now a Jockey Club handicapper, Anthony Winlaw, thought I might have some fun with it at no great expense.

"Expense" had become a relative term, since, in the eighteen years between my first involvement with racehorse-owning and now, even the fees at the lowest end of the scale had gone up from eleven guineas a week to nearer one hundred. Trainers like Henry Cecil and Guy Harwood, with their mainly Arab clientele, charged twice that amount. Prize money had certainly improved, but far from correspondingly.

The owner, David thought, would accept £5000 for an immediate sale. At first I dismissed the idea out of hand, but by the end of a sleepless week I began to weaken. The horse in question was a seven-year-old gelding by Bend a Bow, who had been runner-up in the Kentucky Derby to the legendary Seattle Slew. He was called, rather unkindly, Round the Twist, and had fallen many times in his first two seasons.

To break even in 1983 – and I certainly could not afford to do much worse – you needed to win something in the region of £5000 in a season, a figure managed by very few jumpers indeed. Round the Twist was due to run in a fortnight's time, in a race in which David said he was reasonably handicapped. He was apparently in good shape, his jumping more reliable. I thought hard about the consequences, but the old fever steadily undermined my resistance. After all, if he was no good, I could always – unless he broke his neck – resell him. He would give me more exercise and fresh air than a picture. Also, I told myself consolingly, it would be a help to David not to lose the horse out of his yard.

I acquired Round the Twist on 9 November, having put the finances in the hands of my friend John Synge at the Redfern Gallery, and on a lovely autumn day at Plumpton two weeks later Liz and I watched Richard Rowe ride him to victory in the Peter Cazalet Memorial Trophy, a race worth £2000. In January, this time ridden by Hywel Davies, he won again at Plumpton, a much sterner race of similar value, and in April, after two disappointing runs in between, the £3000 Abergavenny Challenge Cup, also at Plumpton. When he was turned out for the summer soon afterwards, he had earned £7000 in prize money and trebled in value.

The next season, ridden by Peter Double, he won two more good races, at Windsor and Plumpton, as well as being placed several times in good company at Chepstow and Worcester. He now jumped flawlessly and, though a timid, solitary horse at home, raced with the utmost courage.

At this stage, Round the Twist, an almost black animal with impeccable manners, was just about the best bargain of my racing life. But now the luck turned with a vengeance. Just before the 1985/6 season was due to start he developed tendon trouble in training and the vet advised a year's rest. He came back the following season but at this point the stable developed a virus and all David's horses ran listlessly for several months. By the time of the 1987 Easter meeting at Plumpton Twist finally seemed back to full fitness and we entered him for the Abergavenny Challenge Cup he had won three years earlier.

The race began well and by the half-way stage he had worked his way towards the front, looking dangerous. Then, within a few strides, it was all over. Jumping slightly short, he somehow contrived as he landed to put his off fore into a hole. Going flat out, the whole weight of him bore down on the awkwardly placed leg. It did not take a second's look to know there was no hope and he was put down immediately.

Plumpton had been by far my most successful racecourse; now it was the saddest.

For someone like myself, born in India and then sent away, the need to identify with a place and to call it home is compelling. For a writer it is doubly so. Although I have spent more of my time in London, the emotional centre of my universe has always been Sussex; not Belloc's or Kipling's Sussex nor Bloomsbury's either, but somewhere between all of them, geographically as well as spiritually. The Sussex in my mind has white Saxon roads and Roman villas, squat downland churches with steep roofs and shingled spires that rise from encircling yews. The wall paintings, as at Clayton and Westmeston, will have been the work of Cluniac monks boarded at Lewes. It is a Sussex painted by William Nicholson and Eric Ravilious, the Downs flaring and scooped, sea in the air and in the light. The landscape flows and brakes, chalk-slashed, tree-shadowed, its lanes dusty, partings in squares of corn. Sheep graze on the foothills, where barns, once thatched, now tiled, catch the westering sun.

The road that winds from east to west below the north slope of the Downs, from Clayton to Lewes and the Cuckmere valley one way, to Chichester and Goodwood the other, runs through all my memories. The Downs themselves veer and flap, billow and fade, above it, as if sailing. Or else take the shape of a woman, nakedly reclining, all secret folds in a green, fertile expansiveness.

Except along the coast it does not change much, year by year, decade by decade; the Roman feeling survives as does the French flavour, though this is kept at bay by sturdy Sussex agriculture. The changes are all seasonal; lush green to ochre and then gale-swept bareness.

As well as its church, so modest from the outside, so rich within, and its castellated railway tunnel, Clayton possesses an archetypally beautiful cricket ground. The wickets may be nothing special, but as you bat and field the Downs enfold you. The two windmills spike the skyline and beneath them, grouped like fielders, browse the black-and-white cattle that appear in so many William Nicholson paintings. Ben, too, did several drawings of the Downs but, in keeping with his general fastidiousness, there are no untidy cows in them. Clayton's semi-abstract disposition of church, barn, flint walls, duck pond and farm cottages, placed just so against the Wolstone-bury beeches, would, however, have been to Ben's taste. Nikolaus Pevsner in his Sussex volume of *The Buildings of England* gives high praise to the church's eleventh-century chancel, while he describes the wall paintings as "unique in England for their extent, preservation and date". Whatever their merit, the Matsfield Arms, opposite Clayton Tunnel, tended to attract greater interest from visiting cricket teams.

From 1972, until we left in 1978, I played cricket regularly for the village, something I had never been able to do during the previous twenty years when work claimed my Saturdays. Our team was no longer composed entirely of locals, since there were not enough of these; the numbers were made up by the odd solicitor, estate agent or local government worker from Brighton.

It was not always so, for in the early days of the club, in the

1890s, the farm, the rectory and the railway provided a full side: four Russells, three Woolers, the Reverend Lionel Shand, Farmer George King and a couple of platelayers lodged in the tunnel house. King supplied the ground and a horse to pull the roller. Tom Key, the assistant secretary when the club was formed, was still the auditor in the 1970s and we still had Russells and Woolers. Ted Wilkins, our slow bowler during my playing days, had been with the club for forty-five years. Harry Knight, opening batsman and secretary, held that position for thirty-five years. The same names appeared year after year, sometimes with devastating results. In 1947 and 1949 Clayton won 19 out of its 26 matches, George Russell taking 125 wickets at an average of 3.7 in 1947. Even in the 1970s there were only three or four of us who were not in some way related to those early Woolers and Russells, and the Mottrams who succeeded them.

Once a year, during my ten-year Presidency of the club, I got up a team to play the village. These were enjoyably old-style and close-fought encounters, the club history once recording that the President's XI included "a county cricketer, a novelist, a cartoonist, an actor, an art dealer, a banker, an archaeologist, a mechanic and a beekeeper". George Cox, the greatest Sussex cricketer never to play for England, appeared several times, as did Gordon Smyth. Mark Boxer, Robert Powell, Simon Raven, Ian Scott-Kilvert and Terry Kilmartin were others who turned out. Julian Symons, whose son Mark was a regular, umpired on occasion, as did John Betjeman and Cuthbert Worsley. Deirdre Connolly's son Simon, by her first marriage, also played, with the Connollys and William Plomer in attendance. My son Jonathan, who never touched a cricket ball from one year to another, frequently bowled the villagers out, to both his and their astonishment. Sometimes there would be sheep and cowpats in the outfield, and Daisy, when I was batting, used to insist on taking up a position at square leg, from which she declined to be moved.

Hugh de Selincourt's and A. G. Macdonell's accounts of village cricket matches, describing an apparently cosier and vanished prewar world, surprisingly date less than one would expect. No doubt Harold Pinter's cricket teams experience the same problems of punctuality, intemperance, and performance. Squires, colonels, clergymen and blacksmiths may be less prominent in the composition of local sides but the social mixture remains as rich.

Sometimes, on certain evenings in London, I imagine I hear the distant rumble of Brighton-bound trains hurtling through Clayton Tunnel. I know it is an illusion, but the sound is immured in me, as once were the hooting of trains over Howrah Bridge, the sirens of Bengal river steamers, the cawing of crows. The noise sets the night into ferment, restoring the past as if it were animated, like the murals in Clayton church. Others may live in the village now, but the beeches still turn for me, clouds lighten along the skyline, summer days promise.

Harvill Paperbacks are published by Collins Harvill,
a Division of the Collins Publishing Group

1. Giuseppe Tomasi di Lampedusa *The Leopard*
2. Boris Pasternak *Doctor Zhivago*
3. Alexander Solzhenitsyn *The Gulag Archipelago 1918-1956*
4. Jonathan Raban *Soft City*
5. Alan Ross *Blindfold Games*
6. Joy Adamson *Queen of Shaba*
7. Vasily Grossman *Forever Flowing*
8. Peter Levi *The Frontiers of Paradise*
9. Ernst Pawel *The Nightmare of Reason*
10. Patrick O'Brian *Joseph Banks*
11. Mikhail Bulgakov *The Master and Margarita*
12. Leonid Borodin *Partings*
13. Salvatore Satta *The Days of Judgment*
14. Peter Matthiessen *At Play in the Fields of the Lord*
15. Alexander Solzhenitsyn *The First Circle*
16. Homer, translated by Robert Fitzgerald *The Odyssey*
17. George MacDonald Fraser *The Steel Bonnets*
18. Peter Matthiessen *The Cloud Forest*
19. Theodore Zeldin *The French*
20. Georges Perec *Life A User's Manual*
21. Nicholas Gage *Eleni*
22. Eugenia Ginzburg *Into the Whirlwind*
23. Eugenia Ginzburg *Within the Whirlwind*
24. Mikhail Bulgakov *The Heart of a Dog*
25. Vincent Cronin *Louis and Antoinette*
26. Alan Ross *The Bandit on the Billiard Table*
27. Fyodor Dostoyevsky *The Double*
28. Alan Ross *Time Was Away*
29. Peter Matthiessen *Under the Mountain Wall*
30. Peter Matthiessen *The Snow Leopard*
31. Peter Matthiessen *Far Tortuga*
32. Jorge Amado *Shepherds of the Night*
33. Jorge Amado *The Violent Land*
34. Jorge Amado *Tent of Miracles*
35. Torgny Lindgren *Bathsheba*
36. Antæus *Journals, Notebooks & Diaries*
37. Edmonde Charles-Roux *Chanel*
38. Nadezhda Mandelstam *Hope Against Hope*
39. Nadezhda Mandelstam *Hope Abandoned*
40. Raymond Carver *Elephant and Other Stories*
41. Vincent Cronin *Catherine, Empress of All the Russias*
42. Federico de Roberto *The Viceroys*

43. Yashar Kemal *The Wind from the Plain*
44. Yashar Kemal *Iron Earth, Copper Sky*
45. Yashar Kemal *The Undying Grass*
46. Georges Perec *W or the Memory of Childhood*
47. Antæus *On Nature*
48. Roy Fuller *The Strange and the Good*
49. Anna Akhmatova *Selected Poems*
50. Mikhail Bulgakov *The White Guard*
51. Lydia Chukovskaya *Sofia Petrovna*
52. Alan Ross *Coastwise Lights*
53. Boris Pasternak *Poems 1955-1959 and An Essay in Autobiography*
54. Marta Morazzoni *Girl in a Turban*
55. Eduardo Mendoza *City of Marvels*
56. Michael O'Neill *The Stripped Bed*
57. Antæus *Literature as Pleasure*
58. Margarete Buber-Neumann *Milena*
59. Yury Dombrovsky *The Keeper of Antiquities*